OUT OF THE BLUES

My Journey Through Depression and Post-Traumatic Stress

SHARRAN MAKIN

First published by Ultimate World Publishing 2024
Copyright © 2024 Sharran Makin

ISBN

Paperback: 978-1-923123-70-0
Ebook: 978-1-923123-71-7

Sharran Makin has asserted her rights under the Copyright, Designs and Patents Act 1988 to be identified as the author of this work. The information in this book is based on the author's experiences and opinions. The publisher specifically disclaims responsibility for any adverse consequences which may result from use of the information contained herein. Permission to use information has been sought by the author. Any breaches will be rectified in further editions of the book.

All rights reserved. No part of this publication may be reproduced, stored in or introduced into a retrieval system, or transmitted in any form, or by any means (electronic, mechanical, photocopying, recording or otherwise) without the prior written permission of the author. Any person who does any unauthorised act in relation to this publication may be liable to criminal prosecution and civil claims for damages. Enquiries should be made through the publisher.

Cover design: Ultimate World Publishing
Layout and typesetting: Ultimate World Publishing
Editor: James Salmon
Cover Image Copyrights: chanchai howharn-Shutterstock.com

Ultimate World Publishing
Diamond Creek,
Victoria Australia 3089
www.writeabook.com.au

TESTIMONIALS

A supportive and enjoyable read for those who have had to rebuild life. This book gave me hope and direction to pick up and forge forward.

Out of the Blues was a read that acknowledged the realism of PTSD. It expressed renewal and a pathway of hope and application to start over and forgive the past.

Thank you Sharran for your truth and honesty for when authority has let you down. Out of the Blues was a tool to start back and renew a damaged soul of PTSD. It gave me courage and forgiveness to start over and tread a better path of life. For this I am so grateful for your pearls of wisdom and insight to recovery.

AA

SHARRAN MAKIN

Sharran's experiences during her childhood in Anna Bay and at Nelson Bay HS has a kind of golden glow about it - involving scuba-diving - then saw her ultimately work for the police, experience marriage and children - and PTSD. From the time when everything seemed to be falling apart, to the re-building, to Sharran now, as a noted photographer and artist. A woman happy within herself and grateful for her life and the elements which have assisted her regain her life. Her story outlines her steps to recovery as a kind of sign post for others.

Jim Kable

DEDICATION

I dedicate this book to my two sons. I am very proud of the men you have both become today. You are the reason I am the strong and loving woman I am today; you gave me the determination not to give up, to continually learn and change so that I could be the best version of myself and, in turn, the best mum I could be. This gives me hope that others can do the same and become the best version of themselves so that this world can become a better place for you and future generations. Never stop learning and improving and never give up hope, knowing that there is always a solution to anything. Most of all, fill your hearts with so much love that it overflows and touches everyone around you, bringing joy to others and making a difference in this world.

I also dedicate this book to the beautiful friends and family who stood by my side during my recovery, giving me hope to keep going, as well as the beautiful former Police Officers who didn't even know me and who volunteered their time to help out and support one of their own. (It is such a shame that the Police Force closed down the program that Police Legacy ran, it was the one thing that they got right. Now, many are missing out on this, and I would have also volunteered as I could see the benefits it brought.) Also deserving of a mention are the doctors and counsellors who did not give up on me and who were capable of thinking outside the box with my recovery.

Finally, I dedicate this book to all those who are suffering from depression, anxiety, post-traumatic stress, and other health challenges at the moment and need a bit of hope and inspiration. I know it is a difficult and long journey for you, and I congratulate you for getting this far. Keep putting one foot in front of the next, make those small changes each day, and get creative with your recovery. You will get there.

CONTENTS

Testimonials	iii
Dedication	v
Chapter 1: Introduction	1
Chapter 2: Ordinary Girl, Far From Ordinary Life	9
Chapter 3: The Nightmare Begins	21
Chapter 4: The Nightmare Continues	33
Chapter 5: The 12-Point Survival Plan	43
Chapter 6: Thinking Outside the Square with My Recovery	63
Chapter 7: Finding the Missing Piece in the Puzzle	79
Chapter 8: The Power of Neuroplasticity	97
Chapter 9: Art as Therapy, The Three P's	107
Chapter 10: Faith and Religion	119
Chapter 11: Reflecting On the Positives and Learnings	137
Chapter 12: Making this World a Better Place	165
Afterword	179
About the Author	183
Find Out More About the Author	185
Disclaimer	187

Chapter I

INTRODUCTION

Once upon a time, I was in the pursuit of offenders. Now, however, after suffering the effects of Post-Traumatic Stress Disorder (PTSD) and depression due to many years of policing, I am in the pursuit of happiness like so many others who have served their community, state, or country as law enforcers, military officers, or emergency service workers. Although PTSD and depression statistics are high for police officers, they affect many people in our community, and those people come from all walks of life and all professions.

I take my hat off to those who have suffered from this debilitating illness, and I wish you and your loved ones all the best with your recovery and future. It is quite a big deal for me to share my journey with you, with all my ups and downs, as it is pretty personal. However, not sharing it would be a tragedy, as many are unnecessarily suffering today in a broken system and losing hope.

There are a number of things that I hope to achieve by sharing my journey with you. The first is that you will find that little ray of hope and something that will help you or your loved ones with the journey of recovery from depression, anxiety, or PTSD. Secondly, I hope that sharing my journey creates more compassion and empathy in the world and helps others who may not have experienced this debilitating illness to understand it better. Finally, I want to make a change for the better in our communities and encourage our leaders, teachers, scientists, police, emergency services, doctors, hospitals, or anyone in our communities who can make a difference to think outside the box and approach challenges and the way they offer support differently.

I planned on writing this book a long time ago. However, I never got a chance to do so, as I have spent many years trying to rehabilitate myself not just with depression but chronic pain and also brain damage (you see, due to treatment I received and my condition many years back, I could not even write my name, I couldn't read or write, use a computer, I lost all the basic survival skills such as cleaning and navigating and remembering people and

INTRODUCTION

places etc.). Oh, and most importantly, I was also bringing up my children as a single mum.

I have had quite the journey and have learned much through my experiences. I am now seeing so many people suffering from the effects of a broken system and the difficulties of current world events such as dealing with coronavirus, conflict and wars across the globe and even within their communities and families, natural disasters, and the impacts of the cost of living. I am also hearing about the massive increase in the number of people now dealing with depression and anxiety and either seeking medication or self-medicating. I hate seeing others suffering unnecessarily, and although I am no longer a police officer, I still have the desire to protect and help others, and that is why I have pushed myself and challenged myself to write this book and get the information out as soon as possible. Right now, there are more people than ever in need of some helpful tips, a little hope and the knowledge that they are not alone.

In this book I will share with you the journey I went through to try to get better and heal. The frustrations I felt when I put my faith in the doctors to heal, only to find that the medications and treatments I was given made me worse. I will share simple strategies and information that the doctors don't share with their patients to help them better manage their health, and explore how certain foods can have an impact on your wellbeing and mental health.

I am not writing this for fame or fortune, nor am I complaining about life or people being cruel or unfair. I am writing because I care about people, want to improve this world, and encourage everyone to do the same. I am also writing from a place of love when I mention some things that have happened, and have simplified many situations, as I don't want to run anyone down or hurt anyone by sharing the whole story. I have had to share certain things so that you can understand the journey I have been through, better understand yourself and others, and think of ways you can support someone you know or a loved one to make this world a better place. It has not been written out of hurt or anger or to make anyone feel guilty.

Unfortunately, my friends and family did not have the knowledge they needed at the time to help me through my journey, and it was not like having a broken arm that heals in months; my illness went on way longer. I believe anyone I mention did the best they could, given their circumstances and that if they knew more, things might have been different. Even to those who are no longer in my life and those who have hurt me deeply, I choose to remember the good times we shared and decide to hold onto the love we shared rather than the hurt. If you identify with something that you could have done differently for yourself or a loved one, I ask you not to feel guilty; however, use it to learn and grow and to become a better version of yourself. I also want

INTRODUCTION

to respect my family and friends, so I do not mention names. I won't go into detail about my work and will try to keep it brief, as there is more than enough negativity and bad things happening in the world, and I am trying to encourage healing and happiness. Even though I may mention something terrible that occurred, I will also state the positives, something I have learned or something good that came from it.

As the saying goes, "We are all in this together". Look out for one another, love one another, and learn how to communicate better, not just now during these difficult times, but always.

I hope that sharing my journey with you helps you through those tough times and gives you hope. Whilst my story may be different to all of you, I have already been through what many people in many countries are now facing for the first time in their lives due to the recent challenges with the coronavirus pandemic – even though it is not as prominent in the news and in conversations as it was several years ago, when we were going through lockdowns. The fact is there are many people still suffering today from the impacts of this virus. Many people are still suffering from long-term health issues, the death of loved ones, the loss of social contact with others, the breakdown of families and friendships, financial hardships and struggles with depression and anxiety. For those of you who have already had challenges of illness, PTSD, depression or anxiety in your lives, let me remind you that we have got this; we have already been through this and survived. We may all still have scars, but we are still here, and the world is a better place for it. I encourage you to share the skills and wisdom you have already learned with others and remind them that it is such a beautiful and comforting feeling to know that someone has your back, so remember to check in on each other.

I also ask that you be patient with me; my spelling and grammar may not be perfect. In fact, it is perfectly imperfect, just like me. Remember, not so long ago, I couldn't read and write. This is a massive stretch for me, and I am doing my best; the message is more important than the grammar. I have also kept the book shorter than most books as I am aware that when we are going through tough times, are unwell or have learning difficulties, concentration can be difficult. It is often easier if things are shorter and more manageable so we don't get overwhelmed.

If you are struggling, please seek help, whether it is from a professional, a friend or family member, Lifeline, Beyond Blue, or another helpline in your area or for your needs. Most of all, don't give up; keep searching, think outside the box, and you will find the correct answers.

INTRODUCTION

PEARLS OF WISDOM:

Choose Faith Over Fear

And

Hope Over Hopelessness

Chapter 2

ORDINARY GIRL, FAR FROM ORDINARY LIFE

I was just an ordinary girl who ended up having a far-from-ordinary life. I came from a loving family and lived with my mum and dad, and my younger brother and sister. Besides moving house a little too much, I had a fantastic childhood. Most of it was spent growing up on a farm that overlooked a beautiful river and then a beachside suburb where the ocean and I became great friends.

The farm was along the riverfront at Hinton. My brother and I would ride our bikes, the motorbike, and the pony. We felt a sense of freedom and had incredible adventures.

We would discover all sorts of things, including old books and bottles, skulls, insects, birds, animals, spiders, fish and eels and secret hideouts. We let our imaginations run wild and invented various games and fun play activities. We made cubby houses in the shed from bales of hay and made a raft from old 40-gallon drums, some wood and ropes we found lying around the farm, with the grand plan of sailing it down the river so we could have lots of adventures, just like Huck Finn did. This may have scared our parents a little – OK, a lot – and we were in so much trouble when they discovered what we were up to.

There was always something to do, and all sorts of activities were happening at the farm, from growing hay, pumpkins, and watermelons to milking cows and collecting eggs. My dad was a police officer, and my parents ran many businesses from the farm, including a hire car business, a bobcat and tipper hire, making gates, and a demolition yard. We would help our parents on the farm and with their businesses, and there was always something to do, always something going on. One of my favourite jobs was helping Dad make farm gates, which he would sell.

We even had racehorses. I can remember the day when my very tall, well-built dad had to race his trotting horse as the driver called in sick; he looked so different to all the other shorter and lighter drivers/jockeys. Everyone probably thought to themselves, "We have got this, there is no way Mako will win, he has never raced before, and we are so much lighter than he is". Wow, did they have it wrong. Dad won his race; I really admired his ability to believe he could do and achieve anything.

One of my favourite memories was when we would sneak off down the paddock and raid the watermelons. We would throw them on the ground so that they smashed open, and then we would hoe into it, and the sticky, sweet juices would run down our faces; we made such a mess. We probably wasted so much food, as there was no way we could have eaten a whole watermelon, but we didn't think about that at the time; we were just kids. The watermelons we have available to us today in our shops are nowhere near as yummy as they were back then as they have been genetically modified so that we, the consumers, don't have to put up with the seeds (I think I prefer them to have the seeds and the great taste). In the last year of living on the farm, we were blessed with the arrival of my little sister, and life got even busier with a new baby in the house.

My parents packed us all up, and we were made to say goodbye to the beautiful friends we had made there. We moved to a beachside suburb in Port Stephens at Anna Bay. Initially, the move was quite challenging, as we had moved to a tourist spot in the middle of the most extended school holidays, during Christmas. I had no friends and felt so alone; making friends during this time was very hard as everyone I spoke to on the beach was on holiday. Eventually, I came across a beautiful girl who laughed when I asked her if she was a tourist or local, thinking it was such an odd question. I was so excited when she said she was a local and was the same age as me. She became a dear friend and helped me navigate my new terrain, introducing me to lots of new people who later became my friends.

Mum and Dad were extremely busy as they had a bottle shop, a news agency, a general store and later, a pizza shop. Reflecting on it now, I wish they had spent more time with us as kids instead of always working. However, I also know they did their best at the time as loan interest rates had gone up to a whopping 17%, and they had no choice but to work long hours if they were to keep our home and business. If I wasn't at school or helping in the shop, I was off going on adventures or riding my bike. I was very blessed as there was so much to see and do, just the place for the creative little adventurer that I was. I would walk through the bush and discover many different plants, animals, and skulls. I would trek through the dunes, climb over the rocks, and walk along the beach, and I just loved swimming in the ocean; here, I would always feel peace, strong and free. When I was old enough, I started scuba diving and discovered a new world under the sea; it was just the best, with many things to see and discover. It was where I felt I truly belonged and was at home. I can relate to the

ORDINARY GIRL, FAR FROM ORDINARY LIFE

Disney Song, Under the Sea, which says, "The human world is really a mess. Life under the sea is better than anything they have up there."

I was an average student who passed all her grades. However, I was an above-average student in my interaction with the community. I did hundreds of hours of volunteer work, helping those in need by giving first aid through my work with the St. John's Ambulance Brigade and volunteering at a local nursing home. I raised money for many charities and worked part-time at the local store, news agency, bottle shop and a local restaurant.

After leaving school, I started my own business. I had a clothing business and then a printing business. I was only 18 years old, had no formal education in the field, and was running my own business. I look back now and think how brave I was to take on this task; what else could you expect from me at the time? I was following in my dad's footsteps. Unfortunately, after everything I have been through, I am not quite as fearless as I was back then. During that time, I was an active member of the local Chamber of Commerce and was the youngest member to be in that position. I enjoyed my time as a business owner. However, something was missing in my life. I had a desire to help others. I had met many police officers along my journey; my father and uncle had been one, and my boyfriend's dad was also one. I believed if I was a policewoman, I could make a difference in the world, make it a better place for my family and community, and help people.

So, in 1994, I left my business, family, friends, and home to become a police officer. The training was intense, both physically and mentally. I wasn't the same as many other students who hung out at the bar in their spare time. I spent my spare time keeping up with my fitness and studies and having adventures abseiling and caving at night with some of my fellow students and friends. It was only on the odd occasion that we would make it to the local watering hole at Tully Park.

The hard work paid off, and I was later sworn in as a police officer. I felt proud to wear the uniform, and I was a hard worker, always going that extra mile and making extra patrols if I ever had some downtime. I always attempted to do the best work possible and wanted to make a difference in my community. I believe I was firm but fair. I treated everyone with respect, including the offenders. However, I also possessed authority and sternness when needed.

If an offender was decent and treated me with respect, they deserved the same. I have an entire folder of letters of appreciation from members of the public thanking me for the work and the support that I did in the community whilst I was a police officer; I even have a letter from the owner of the house that I helped detectives search in a surprise raid. They commended me for my excellent work and the respect I showed during such difficult times (I can only think that maybe they were treated poorly in the past by the police, as I was only doing my job). There were many boxes of thank you letters during the year I worked as a road education officer.

Most of my policing was general duties, though I also worked for several years as a police youth liaison officer, working with young offenders and children at risk. Due to my excellent communication skills and my bubbly personality, I would often be chosen to represent the police at community events or give a talk to the public.

Eventually, my time protecting my community took its toll on me, and with post-traumatic stress disorder, my bubbly personality disappeared, and depression set in. I had managed to keep the water calm for much of my career. There were a few large swells that would come from time to time. However, they would settle, and the waters became calm again. Then suddenly, without warning and without being able to do anything to stop it, a massive tsunami hit, taking me and my emotions with it. Life as I knew it was over and would never return. Where I once believed I could help make a difference in the world, I realised that there was too much red tape, too many ridiculous barriers, too many rules, and too many senior officers blocking changes that needed to happen.

I started a few community projects but was hitting roadblock after roadblock. I organised a touch football game with youth and children in the community in an area identified as having a high risk of offending. When my supervisor ordered me not to do it anymore, there were complaints from the Aboriginal elders and others in the community as they had noticed that what I was doing was making a difference. I was determined not to give up on these kids, so I went and played touch football with them in my own time and not as part of my shift. I really did want to make a difference with these kids and not give up on them as so many in their lives had already done. When word got back to my supervisor that I was still running the touch football games, even though it was in my own time, I was told to stand down. I was only trying to improve their lives and give them hope so they would make good choices rather than turn to crime and be at risk, making our community a better place.

It was hard to do my job as a youth liaison officer; I felt blocked from many angles. I was expected to attend meetings, interact with the community and schools, attend youth justice conferences, deliver cautions, work with the schools to engage at-risk children, reduce truanting, engage with young offenders, and perform many other duties. I would organise meetings and events to attend only to discover that I could not get a vehicle; frustrated at wanting to do my job well, I started driving my car when one wasn't available. Wow, I certainly got into trouble when my supervisor found out. Enough was enough, though, when I identified a number of children at risk of sexual abuse in our community who needed help and protection from several predators who were also living in the community.

At the time, I only worked part-time and knew I had to keep up with my regular duties, but I also knew these kids needed protection. Knowing that overtime wouldn't be supported, I set to work, putting in many hours of my own time and gathering all the information and intelligence I needed to present to my supervisors. I was so disappointed when I was told to stand down; I took things to the next level of authority but was told to stand down again and again. It broke me knowing that these kids needed my help, and I couldn't help them.

All the pressures of being a police officer built up over time, until there was an incident that caused a bubble to burst, or was it the straw that broke the camel's back? I had two young boys myself; if I couldn't protect the kids in my community, how was I going to protect my kids? My whole world started to spin, and I could feel my health and well-being tumbling. Before I got knocked down, there was no way I was going down without a fight. As a last resort, I sent all the information I had gathered to all the relevant child protection agencies, hoping it would make a difference, and then I crumbled. I felt helpless and worthless, wanting to help but unable to; I could not wear the uniform again. Years later, I discovered it was much bigger than I had imagined. This had happened on a much larger scale, not only in my area but across all of Australia, and a Royal Commission into child sexual abuse was established.

Ten years later, I felt wounded yet again and felt a vast stabbing pain in my heart. Panic filled my body, and there was a flooding of tears that gushed from my eyes when I awoke to my morning alarm radio and heard the news report on the Royal Commission, stating that several suspects that I had identified in my intelligence gathering had been arrested for paedophilia. There was a sense of relief, but also anger, at how many other young children may have fallen prey to these offenders during those ten years that had passed. I felt sorry for my son, who was asleep nearby that morning, as my intense sobbing had woken him, and he had become worried about his mum. I no longer wake up to the radio and the depressing state of affairs of the news after that incident.

Physically and mentally, I was exhausted; my body had shut down, and I could not leave the door to work. I tried and tried, but I could not do it; I needed a break. I thought at the time I was doing the right thing by visiting the doctor, as nothing like this had ever happened to me. I later learned that this may not have been my wisest decision.

PEARLS OF WISDOM:

Be like a chameleon, able to adapt and change to the world around you; always looking forward yet observing from behind. (Sharran Makin)

My health may fail, and my spirit may grow weak, but God remains the strength of my heart; he is mine forever. (Ps 73:26)

Chapter 3

THE NIGHTMARE BEGINS

My treatment for depression and PTSD has been quite the journey. When I first realised my depression had become so bad that I could no longer force myself to go to work as a police officer anymore, I went to my GP, and there the slippery slope began. I had always believed doctors were wise, knew much more about things than I did, and could help and heal anyone. If I got sick, the pharmacy and doctors would heal and help me recover. I was very wrong.

Please don't take me the wrong way. I'm not bagging doctors, pharmacists, or medicine; our medical system has advanced in many ways, but in many ways, it has also slipped backwards. There is so much more to be learned and to be discovered. Remember, people once believed that the Earth was not round and that if you travelled too far, you would fall off the edge. Back then, they thought they had all the answers, and no one could prove them wrong. They were proved wrong.

It was back in my parent's generation that doctors encouraged you to smoke, that it would make your health and your life better. Many, many years back, they even used to smoke tobacco enemas in people's bums. That's literally where the term "blowing smoke out of your arse" came from; back then, they said it would cure all sorts of illnesses, and could even stave off death. Now, they have discovered that tobacco is nasty for our health and can cause death. We used to have a considerable tobacco industry here in Australia some time ago. We once grew and manufactured tobacco; however, there have been no licenced growers since 2006 or manufacturers since 2015, and it is now illegal to do so because it is terrible for people's health.

I believe many years from now, the insurance companies and medical system will look back on the way they have treated many people suffering from depression and post-traumatic stress, and they will find that they have made many patients' health worse and that they have also contributed to many deaths. They will realise

THE NIGHTMARE BEGINS

that they could have done things differently regarding mental health and learn that many things they did, did more harm than good.

We can see all sorts of evidence of this. If we look back upon medical history, it was during the late '40s and early '50s that medical procedures were occurring, where doctors stuck an ice-pick through somebody's eyeball to sever a part of their brain so they could not feel emotions. Oh, my goodness, how barbaric is that? And how many people and families had to suffer from this horrible treatment. Fortunately, it was later banned.

There is an excellent movie based on a true story called NISE: The Heart of Madness (2015), about Dr Nise da Silveira, a Brazilian psychiatrist who tried to put a stop to this treatment and electric shock treatment to psychiatric patients who realised that patients responded better with nurturing, art, nature, music, and community. She did beautiful work with her patients, and her treatment worked way better than the brutal treatment other doctors were giving. Some doctors did not like the work she was doing and the success she was having and tried to sabotage her hard work and limit her patient's improvements so that they could get the glory and more work. I won't give too much away as it is a movie worth seeing. When I watched it, I realised I had already discovered all this and included these techniques in my healing plan. It reinforced that I was undoubtedly on the right track.

I wish I had never met my first psychologist; I had gone to him for help with my depression and PTSD. Instead, he made my health, my depression, and my life way worse. I trusted him, and he let me down. I did not realise this at the time because the medicine he gave me was mucking up my ability to process things and problem-solve to realise that the treatment wasn't helping me, but rather harming me. When I got worse, he told me that it was just my depression and post-traumatic stress getting worse, and he increased my medication and added new stuff. I listened and obeyed like a good little patient, believing he knew what he was doing. I didn't realise at the time the medication was making me worse. Do your research into drugs to treat depression, anxiety, and PTSD; you will find that they all have some side effects. Some can be serious, and some increase your chances of getting cancer, diabetes, anxiety, depression, weight gain, suicidal thoughts, and a whole range of other side effects. It is scary, and so is experiencing these side effects.

After many years of treatment with this doctor, I was on so many different medicines and at very high doses. I couldn't function. I could not be a mum, I could not be a wife, and I could not be a friend, a sister, or a daughter. I couldn't be anything; my head was such a mess, my body was a mess, and my life was a mess. I put on 30 kilograms as a side effect of this medication. Everything was so messy, and I had become so unwell that I spent at least ten months or more in psychiatric hospitals over

THE NIGHTMARE BEGINS

three years, being away from my family and my friends. During those three years of being admitted into the hospital, I was subjected to so much torture, including the over prescription of medicines and electric shock treatment to the brain (ECT). Yes, electric shock treatment to the brain. ECT is still around today.

My family and I were told there were minimal side effects to these treatments at the time. Just a little bit of memory loss around the time of receiving treatment, but no long-term memory loss. We were also told that it would be good for me. My parents and husband, at the time, believed what the doctors were telling them. They thought, like many, that the doctors had all the answers, so they began my journey with ECT. I had lots of it on different parts of my brain. I can't even remember much from that period at all. What I can tell you, from what I've been told, is that I was there in body form – which didn't even look like my body – but that I wasn't there in mind and spirit. People would speak to me, and I would stare off into the distance or right through them. My youngest son told me that he visited me in the hospital one time, and I didn't even know who he was. The poor kid, it must have been so scary for him seeing his mum like that.

In the end, enough was enough. I'd spent many years trying to get better and only got worse. I had ten months or more stolen from me, away from my family and friends;

they had taken my memory, my life, and my spirit. I had lost my health, and I lost hope. The memory loss was significant; I could not remember anything. I couldn't even write my name or remember where I lived or how old I was, and I could not see any other option but to end my life and my suffering and the suffering of those close to me.

Please don't ever take this point of view. If you or your loved one is struggling, think outside the square and do things differently. Get and give the love and support that is needed. Stand up for yourself and speak out. Sometimes, treatments can make you worse rather than better, so speak up, change doctors if needed, or find another solution.

Didn't I have that wrong? God had other plans for me. He intervened; he had his angels and Earth Angels come to be with me. Due to my state of mind, I was transferred to a more secure hospital. I am very grateful to my dear dad for stepping in at this time; someone had finally realised that the doctor and his treatment were making me worse rather than better. Finally, somebody got it. He found me a new hospital and a new doctor.

Although this doctor did not develop a magical cure that would instantly fix all my problems, I am so grateful that I have him in my life. He's a caring doctor who thinks outside the box. He listens to me and accepts when I say

THE NIGHTMARE BEGINS

that medicine is making me worse rather than better. He respects that I'm trying hard to get better, healthier, and happier. He also respects and encourages me with alternative therapy. He is always looking out for new treatments, whether that be mainstream or alternative medicine or therapy; he is a good man and doctor and realises that I do much better staying away from mainstream medicine.

It was not until my last treatment in the hospital with a new doctor that I realised the extent of my memory loss. He had taken me off all the hard drugs and prescription drugs that my previous doctor had me on; this made me more aware of what was going on around me and just how bad things had become. The hospital gave me a form to fill in. I couldn't do it. I couldn't remember how to spell my name. I didn't know how old I was, I didn't know my date of birth, and I didn't know how to spell where I lived.

From then on, I realised more and more the extent of my memory loss, especially when I returned home to everyday life. I couldn't remember how to drive. I couldn't remember people's names and faces unless I had a strong emotional attachment to them. I couldn't read, write, or work out basic maths. I had lost all sense of place and direction. I couldn't remember how to cook or the basics of housework. I was starting from scratch. It was so terrifying. When I look back now at this journey, I don't know how the doctors and the father of my children had left me with two children to take care of. I am glad they did, though, as they were my inspiration for all my hard work to make sure I improved so I could be the best mum I could be for them.

My new doctor tried so many different medications to try to fix or relieve my depression. Nothing was working; having a break from medication caused me to be more aware of everything around me and my body. This was good; I could let the doctors know how the medicines affected me this time. The side effects were so harmful with most of them, and my body or tummy would not let me take them. Some made me mentally worse – it was scary, and at times caused me to feel suicidal. In the end, I just gave up trying different medications, as I certainly didn't want to be worse than what I was. I was a kind and loving person; I wasn't going to let any medicine turn me into a mean, horrible beast or take my life. I may have still been depressed by not taking medication, but at least I was not harming myself or others, and I could still be a mum. After a few years of doing it on my own, I discovered many things that would help me keep my depression at levels so I could at least go on for the sake of my kids, as they certainly needed me.

Some days were indeed a challenge, and I believe it was only through the grace of God that I've managed to get through them. What a lot of people don't realise is that

THE NIGHTMARE BEGINS

post-traumatic stress changes the structure of your brain and damages it in some way. I had a double whammy as the ECT electric shock to my brain worsened this damage. For some people, ECT has worked, and the side effects have not been as significant as they were for me; I have not met any of these people, and everyone I have spoken to has regretted the decision to get ECT.

For many people like me, it turned out to be their worst nightmare, turning their world upside down and resulting in significant memory loss. There is a Facebook group for victims of electric shock treatment, ECT and TMS magnetic therapy; it is so sad reading their stories and the challenges that they are going through due to the treatment their doctors gave them. It brings up so many bad memories of the challenges I faced. It is so shocking how some of these people have been left after medical treatment. Here I was, an adult left with a child's brain. It was terrifying. Could you imagine leaving your five-year-old child to look after and care for a ten and twelve-year-old on their own? That is what it was like for me as a single mum. Yes, I felt like running away, but I couldn't. My kids needed me.

There were times when I thought that things could not get worse. Already I was suffering from chronic pain, depression, and memory loss – things couldn't get worse than that, could they? Well, just when I thought life had fallen that far, that I had hit the bottom of the cliff, a giant sinkhole opened and sucked me down even further. How could this be possible? I didn't think I could fall any further. Turns out I could. My husband, weeks after I had returned from the hospital, told me he was no longer in love with me and that he wanted to end our marriage. He had found someone else. I had memory loss, depression, and chronic pain. I was learning all the basics again, like reading, writing, driving, cooking, cleaning, navigating, and learning who people and places were. I could hardly look after myself, and here I was, being left a single mum; I could not believe this was happening.

We made a vow to each other to be there in sickness and in health, in poorness and in wealth, and here I was, being left a single mum when I needed my husband more than ever. I was still unwell and had to learn the basics. I was so sick and in survival mode, trying to work out all the basics of life and being able to live and survive and be a single mum. I could hardly look after myself, let alone the kids. Most of my friends also left with my husband; he was the strongest and the healthiest. I couldn't go water skiing or motorbike riding, but he could. I couldn't even drink alcohol or party, but he could. I had to learn all the basics again and how to survive in this very challenging world; I was no fun, and he was.

So many people couldn't understand what was happening under the surface and how difficult things were for me. They could see a woman who could walk and talk, so

THE NIGHTMARE BEGINS

they thought I was okay. I couldn't find anyone to help me. I was so alone. At least kids have teachers and parents to help them learn and grow; this is not so for an adult suffering from memory loss. It is hard and not at all like it is in the movies. I couldn't be like Billy Madison, going back to school to learn with the kids.

A couple of friends stood by me, and I am forever grateful to them. However, they had their own challenges and were very busy with family and work. I felt I couldn't call on them as I didn't want to put extra pressure on them. The year that my husband walked out was challenging not only for me but also for my kids. They were struggling at school and getting up to mischief. I could see the happiness draining out of them. Dealing with discipline and the behaviour of children can be complicated with broken families. I felt like I was all alone and had to work out a solution fast to make sure my kids got back on track. Eventually, with hard work, things did improve.

SHARRAN MAKIN

PEARLS OF WISDOM:

Never regret a day in your life. Good days give you happiness, bad days give you experiences, worst days give you lessons, and best days give you memories. (Unknown)

The Lord is my light and salvation, so why should I be afraid? (Psalms 27:1)

Chapter 4

THE NIGHTMARE CONTINUES

With my new doctor's help, I tried to go on several antidepressants again, and they did make things better for a tiny bit; however, there came a time when I knew that I needed to get off them. My body was shutting down. I had pains in my tummy all the time. Some days, it got so bad that I thought I was dying, and I took myself to the doctors and even the hospital for help, but no one could give me any answers. I was getting ulcers in my mouth, on my tongue, and on my lips. My GP could not give me any answers and gave me a medicine that made it worse. I was getting rashes all over my hands and my arms and random bruises on my body. Some days, I could hardly get out of bed, and there were days that I just had to stop, and I couldn't do anything at all; it was like I had chronic fatigue. No one could help me, no one could give me answers, and I honestly, at the time, thought I was going to die.

Interestingly, God had my back, and the right person entered my life for a short time; he pointed me in the direction of some great articles, documentaries and DVDs, and to an interesting lady who did workshops about food and medicines. Wow, my head was spinning. I was discovering that in some people, certain foods can have really bad side effects on your body and that they were best to be avoided (this information turned out more valuable than gold to me). I learned even simple things like the fact that how a food is prepared also changes its nutritional value. Who would have guessed that instant oats contained more sugar than normal oats? I had no idea that medicines could have such substantial side effects and shut down your body; I now understand it all, and why I've faced such problems during my time of treatment. I was put on three medicines at the time; I'd read an article on one of the medications, and many people were suing the company as they had developed diabetes. I already had a family history of diabetes, and I didn't want to add to my chances of getting it. Doctors could not give me an answer to why my body was shutting down. They couldn't help me, so I had to help myself.

THE NIGHTMARE CONTINUES

OK, I know. I said before that I didn't think things could get any worse, but they did. It turned out that going off three different antidepressants, even with the help of the doctor and even taking it slowly over the year, turned out to be quite the challenge. I honestly believe it's the hardest thing I have ever done. However, it was also the best thing I had ever done. I made sure I only reduced my medication on the days that the kids were staying with their dad, and I knew that I wouldn't have my children around me. This was important, as each time I reduced my medicine, it felt like I was on the scariest ride and was in a terrifying horror story at the same time. I had to shut myself away from the rest of the world to protect myself and others.

It felt like the world was spinning so fast that it was making me feel ill. I felt like I was in a war zone and the enemy was throwing grenade after grenade at me, explosion after explosion. I had no control over my thoughts; I had no control over my body; I was crying continuously; I was so angry; I was so scared; my heart felt like it was pounding so hard that it was about to explode. I could not do anything at all on these days except hide away from the world as every sound, even the sound of a gentle breeze or a car driving past, sounded like the volume was turned up to the maximum sound level that a speaker could take. The sound vibrated through every inch of my body, the light would aggravate me, so there was certainly no shopping on these days as the harsh fluorescent lighting and even the sunlight would feel like it was burning through my very soul.

I even had to choose the clothes I wore carefully, as anything too tight or artificial would make me feel like I was being suffocated and would send me into a panic. It appeared that anything and everything would annoy me, which was very frustrating and exhausting. Reflecting on my experiences as well as the experiences I have heard others go through, it is so scary to think of the possible side effects that so many antidepressants on the market today have. What is even more alarming is that they are designed to keep us as a society addicted. So many people cannot handle the side effects and the disruptions that occur in their lives when reducing medication and instead choose to remain on it. For some, the medication affects and damages their bodies and organs over time, and in time, the medicine may stop working (known as tachyphylaxis). Then they're back to square one, suffering from depression and anxiety once more. NOTE: Please get the support of your doctor when reducing medication; it is dangerous with some medicines to stop taking them abruptly.

That year was one of the most challenging of my life. However, afterwards, being off my medication and changing and controlling my diet, things started to improve. My skin cleared, I had more energy, and if I didn't eat or drink the wrong foods, I could limit or reduce the pains in my tummy and the ulcers in my mouth.

THE NIGHTMARE CONTINUES

Life was still hard dealing with depression. However, it was way better dealing with it off medication than it was on medication. At least I was still alive, and most importantly, I could still be a mum.

Over the years, there have been a few times when things have got on top of me, and I have buckled, and I thought I really do need that magic pill. However, each time I took that magic pill, the side effects were so harmful that I could hardly function, or they turned me into a monster that I wasn't. I had no choice but to stop taking the medicine and return to the loving, kind person that I am. Some medications even made me feel suicidal, which is not in my nature either (luckily, I had become aware of my body and mind and the effects that different medicines and different foods could have on me, so I decided to stop consuming those which impacted me negatively).

I am sorry to anyone who may have crossed my path during such times. Please know that it was not me, but the medication that had changed me. If you or anyone you know experiences this, you must speak to your doctor. If it is someone you know who is being affected by their medicine, please know that that person needs love and support during this difficult time and not for you to back them into a corner and yell at them, criticising them or telling them that they are a bad person, or that there are people worse off than them in this world. It will only make the matter worse.

I am a loving and kind soul; however, some medications can make me or others the opposite. Fortunately, I now know this and can take the required action, but I had no idea what was going on for a while there. Unfortunately, if I do try a new medicine, even an antibiotic, and I do react, I need to wait for the drug to leave my system. What I needed most during those difficult times was to feel loved and held and told everything would be okay, and that someone had my back; tomorrow is a new day, and we will get through this. Unfortunately, at the time, my family did not understand my needs, and they did not understand the effects that some medicines could have on me.

The thing is, now I pretty much deal with things on my own and, on those bad days, keep to myself so that nobody is affected. I simply wait until the medicine or food that I have reacted to leaves my system. The only time my family or anyone else has seen me act poorly is when I have been on or started a new medication or if I have a terrible reaction to an additive or preservative in processed food. The crazy thing is when I would have a bad reaction, they would yell at me, "Go to the doctors and get yourself on medication". Ironically, it was the doctor and the medication causing me to be worse, and they were trying to force me down a path that would make me worse or even die.

I'm just so grateful I became aware of this, as many don't. Looking back on my life, I actually wonder how

THE NIGHTMARE CONTINUES

many people may have been put into the legal system unnecessarily, lost their jobs, been kicked out of school or had families destroyed, either due to medications or drugs they have taken or simply by innocently eating the chemically laden processed food that is part of our everyday food supply. I wonder how many lives have also been lost through these same means. I have helped prevent a few of these simply by sharing my knowledge.

I wish someone had given me this information before I started down the field of being medicated. I really do think my life and journey would have been heaps better and easier. Dealing with depression and anxiety by taking more natural approaches through diet, exercise, meditation, mindfulness etc. is hard work. However, it is so worth it. I also know friends of mine who are medicated, but despite that they still follow the tips I am going to share with you as much as they can, as they find that they can control their condition much better if they do.

I'm not a medical doctor, and if you are on medication, I'm not telling you to go off your prescriptions. Going off medication or reducing medication needs to be done with the help or support of a doctor. I also know some people in my life who use antidepressants, and they say it has helped them with their symptoms. However, I also know many that it has helped, only for it to suddenly stop working, and they find themselves struggling again.

There are also people like me for whom medications can make their symptoms worse. We are all different, and we need to be treated differently. I believe PTSD is one of the more complex conditions to treat. If you or a loved one is getting worse, or simply not getting better, maybe something needs to be changed. Everyone is different; sometimes, we must think outside the box for healing to start.

It is interesting that as I started to heal, more challenges popped up. When my memories initially started returning, it was usually the memories that had strong emotional ties connected to them that returned first. Unfortunately, that meant a lot of my policing memories were returning. I started having nightmares, and I would wake in the middle of the night kicking and screaming. The dreams were so vivid and violent that I could not return to sleep; believe me, no sleep and depression are not a very good combination.

These memories returning caused me to be hyper-vigilant once again. I was always watching my back; if I went out in public, I would constantly be scanning for threats, and I wouldn't go out at night. If I were at home, my doors and windows were always locked. I slept with the alarm on (my kids would have to wake me up in the night if they needed to go to the toilet so I could turn the alarm off), and I had things hidden throughout the house that I could reach easily if I needed to protect myself or my

THE NIGHTMARE CONTINUES

kids. For a while there, I was super protective of my kids, and I didn't want to have them out of my sight. This was OK for a while but became exhausting and wasn't a good way to live. I knew things needed to change, and over time, I worked out ways to deal with this anxiety.

I must admit, though, new challenges presented themselves as my kids grew older. It is challenging enough for parents bringing up teenagers in a world where there is corruption, crime, drugs, alcohol, paedophiles, sex, and a world wide web, and they are also at an age where they are growing, experimenting and pushing the boundaries. Try doing it as a single mum and former police officer with PTSD. Those memories of jobs you attended throughout your career return, the motor vehicle accidents, drug overdoses, bashings, kids underage drinking and turning to crime, knocking on doors and delivering the news that a loved one had died and will not be returning home, and the list goes on.

Believe me, I was in perpetual state of worry for quite a few years, on constant alert. My kids had a mum who watched them like a hawk, although I'm sure a few things did go under the radar, and they got away with a few things like most teenagers do. The good news is that I managed to get them through their teenage years, and at the time of writing this, they are now 23 and 25. I am so proud of the men they have turned into today, and I love them both very much.

PEARLS OF WISDOM:

Life is like a camera. Focus on what is important, capture the good times, and develop from the negatives. If things don't work out, take another shot. (Unknown)

Can all your worries add a single moment to your life? (Matthew 6:27)

Chapter 5

THE 12-POINT SURVIVAL PLAN

Navigating challenging times has taught me invaluable lessons that I'm eager to share. From battling illnesses to grappling with depression, anxiety, and the isolating embrace of solitude, the journey to survival demanded a blend of creativity and resilience. It wasn't just about artistic creativity, although that played a role; it was about crafting innovative solutions, thinking outside the box and embracing trial and error until the correct answers emerged. These 12 points encapsulate the multifaceted approach that guided me through adversity. As we delve deeper into each, I hope you find insights that resonate with your unique journey.

What works for one person may not work for another; sometimes, we need trial and error before we get the correct answer. For me, I certainly needed to do that, as the modern medicine way of solving problems and society's way of solving problems certainly didn't help me; it made me feel worse and nearly killed me. I wasted so much time and money trying to find a way to be well again; I was desperate. Ultimately, these twelve key points illuminated my path to survival and growth, which I will share with you. I hope they also help you or someone you care deeply about.

12-point survival plan

1. Prioritise Quality Sleep

Ensure a good night's sleep, tailoring the hours to your unique needs. Establish sleep-friendly habits, such as avoiding electronic devices post-7:00pm, maintaining a comfortable sleep environment, and being mindful of bedtime.

I feel much better and function better with eight hours of sleep; some people need a little more and some a little less. However, getting a good night's sleep helps the body heal and certainly helps to keep the blues away.

A few things I put in place to ensure this happens include, as I mentioned, staying off my electronic devices, such as my phone, computer, and iPad, after 7:00pm. I noticed I had trouble sleeping if I got on my devices after this time. The other thing I needed to do was make sure that my bed and pillows were comfortable (it took a long time for me to find the perfect pillows). I also ensured that I was not too hot or cold. I made my room dark and got new blinds to block out the light from my night owl neighbours that came through my window. I also tried not to have any caffeine or chocolate after 5:00 PM and not to eat my dinner too late, as eating a meal late mucked up my sleep, and so did skipping my dinner.

Each person has their own unique body clock; I noticed I got the best night's sleep and felt the best if I went to bed between 9:30 and 10:30pm; I noticed if I stayed up too late after midnight, I tended to feel sluggish and down the next day. Become aware of what works best for you and put it into action.

2. Stress Management

Minimise stress by discerning between what's within your control and what isn't. Release the burden of unnecessary worries, focusing energy on addressing manageable challenges.

Yes, I know, sometimes stress can be unavoidable and not our fault. However, we can choose to let go of stressing over unimportant things that we have no control over and find ways to deal with things thrown our way that we do have control over. It takes practice, and don't beat yourself up if you don't get it straight away; we can all make slip-ups occasionally. I admire a couple of friends and have tried to embrace what they do. They concentrate on one day at a time and don't worry about the things going on in the world that they have no control over and cannot change. Being an empath, I tended to get worried about all the bad things happening worldwide. Dolly Parton has a great song, "In the Meantime". When I heard it, I smiled, and it has become one of my favourite songs; she writes about how people have been talking about the end of time ever since time began and she reminds us not to worry.

On those tough days, I often think of the Serenity Prayer:

God, grant me the serenity to accept the things I cannot change, the courage to change things I can, and the wisdom to know the difference.

3. Mindful Eating

Pay attention to your diet, recognising the impact of food on your well-being. Choose fresh, whole foods over processed alternatives and explore what dietary choices resonate with your body's needs.

Now, I'm not telling you to go on a strict diet. However, I suggest you watch what you consume to fuel your body.

THE 12-POINT SURVIVAL PLAN

Some foods will help you thrive, and some will leave you stressed out and feeling like crap and can lead to some dark thoughts, depression, and anxiety.

Some say it's better to become a vegetarian. I can't comment here as I'm not a nutritionist. However, we all have different body types; some function better by having a bit of fish, poultry, and meat (I usually only have red meat once or twice a week as too much doesn't make me function well; however, having none can leave me not working at my best also). I find if I don't have a good amount of protein in my diet, I feel crappy. Determine what works best for you and helps you feel well and thrive.

My body and mind work best by avoiding colours, preservatives and additives where I can. Please do your research into them, and you will be surprised at what they are putting in our food these days; some of them are scary, and some have been linked to cancer and all sorts of other health and behavioural issues. Some colours that I have consumed in the past have caused my depression and anxiety to worsen and caused me to become angry and emotional. When I looked up that food colour, I noticed it was in a lot of our processed foods and beverages and had been linked to head banging and behavioural problems in children, as well as cancer. Knowing that, the food went straight into the bin, there was no way I was leaving it for my sons to consume. I even react to citric acid, an additive in many of today's foods, medicines, and health foods we consume; it looks innocent enough, right? However, it is made in a lab using a type of mould.

Many of our foods have been genetically modified so they are resistant to bugs and pests. The bugs have been smart enough to stay away from the plants; however, we humans have not, and many of us suffer the consequences through allergies and other health problems. There are more and more Australians becoming more sensitive to gluten than ever before. We must ask ourselves why. Is it because our wheat and other plants are getting genetically modified and sprayed with pesticides? Why is it that other countries that don't engage in these practices don't have people suffering from gluten intolerance that other countries do?

We all know the importance of eating fresh fruit and vegetables, right? Yes, fruit and vegetables are essential, and so is trying to get a variety of colours included in your diet. However, some fruits and vegetables may only suit some, and everyone will be different here depending on your body and health. I encourage you all to explore the fruits and vegetables that work best for you to keep you healthy and happy. Some may find when they do a little more digging that they have intolerances to some, and some other people may find that they need to reduce the ones that are high in sugar because of health challenges like diabetes.

THE 12-POINT SURVIVAL PLAN

Limiting certain fruits and vegetables from my diet has been good for me. Unfortunately, having a continual amount of stress has left my body more vulnerable, and some foods I was able to eat before suffering from PTSD now no longer serve me. Things like oranges, pineapple and avocado can leave me with ulcers in my mouth. I also find that things like some mushrooms can give me hives, as can things containing gluten, as well as a swollen belly, a swollen airway, and fatigue. I also reacted to vinegar; I only found out the other day that certain kinds of vinegar contain gluten, something that I wasn't aware of, which probably explains why I reacted to it.

Giving up coffee was also good for me, but as I said, everyone's different. Once I gave coffee away, I realised how much it affected me. It was causing me to have stomach pain, headaches, fatigue and brain fog. I replaced it with tea, which is gentler on my body and mind. Alcohol was another sacrifice for me; when I became more mindful of what I was consuming, I noticed that even the smallest amount of alcohol would send me backwards, and I couldn't function for days. I was never a big drinker, so it wasn't that hard to give up. I have now discovered that I can have a few tequilas from time to time; somehow, it does not affect me like other alcohols do, perhaps because it is pure and doesn't contain gluten, sulphides and other additives like many other alcoholic beverages do. Don't worry, I still have some treats. I like chocolate, and I have found one that does not give me any side effects and tastes great, too.

Yes, I know many won't understand this remedy, as many people out there have high blood pressure and have been told to reduce salt. This is not the case for me and many others out there. Some of us have naturally low blood pressure, and good quality salt, like Celtic salt or Himalayan salt, with the nutrients left in it, are essential to keeping us well and happy. I don't eat a lot of processed food, so I don't have a lot of salt in my diet. I also found that many salts on the market today have been processed, and many nutrients have been stripped. Good salt in my diet certainly helps me, and my blood pressure is now stable.

4. Exercise for Mood Enhancement

Tailor your exercise routine to your capabilities, consulting a healthcare professional if necessary. Understand the symbiotic relationship between physical activity and mood elevation, acknowledging the unique exercise needs dictated by your circumstances.

Exercising is great for my mood. When we exercise, our bodies release multiple hormones, including endorphins and serotonin. It is said to be better than any antidepressant or drug and doesn't have the side effects that they do. Exercise helps with my mood, my cognition, and my concentration. It also gives me more confidence. When

I walk, I often give people I pass a greeting and a smile; not only have I noticed that it improves my mood and helps give me a sense of connection, but I have noticed that others also benefit from it. Exercise has many other health benefits, including improving muscle tone and strength, helping with blood pressure and weight control, and strengthening our hearts. Oddly enough, even though we use more energy, it can also increase our energy levels.

Get creative with your exercise and see what works for you and your health needs. There are all forms of exercise; some can be individual, and others can be done with friends, family, or a team. Some may find swimming or a bike ride more pleasurable than walking. Do what works best for you. Some people may have injuries they must consider, which is undoubtedly the case for me. The primary key here is movement. Even a stream or a river needs to flow to stay healthy.

5. Mindfulness and Meditation

Combat the chaos of a restless mind through mindfulness and meditation. Embrace simplicity in practices, whether focusing on your breath, appreciating nature, or engaging in guided meditations that resonate with your inner self.

Some of you may relate to having a monkey mind that jumps from one thing to another, which can sometimes be hard to control. It can also add to our challenges in dealing with depression and anxiety. I found some relief when I learned to quieten the chatter in my head, it has allowed me to have a deeper connection with friends and loved ones. I would often chat with someone, watch a movie or be in a class, and my mind would jump to something totally unrelated. I would stare off into the distance, and being a visual person, would often have a movie or image playing out in my mind, and I would miss big chunks of information. This can still happen occasionally, but nowhere near as much as it used to. I try not to be too hard on myself and gently remind myself to return to the present and what I am doing.

Learning mindfulness and meditation and practising them regularly helped me stay more focused and calmer. It helped with my memory loss and improved my cognition. The more straightforward meditations, like focusing on my breath, doing a body scan, or progressive muscle relaxation, work best for me. We are all different, and what one person likes may not work for another. Be aware, though, that some meditations can also have the opposite effect. I found that some guided meditations made my anxiety go through the roof and were not at all relaxing; with some, the music and sound would aggravate me, and with others, the voice or the words they spoke would evoke anger or anxiety. I suggest experimenting with what works best for you. If something makes you feel worse rather than better, turn it off and find something that does help you.

We are all different; some people cannot visualise, or specific frequencies can affect them. Some people may not like the destination or things that may be placed in some meditations due to a bad experience from their past, so they may find it stressful if they are sent on a guided meditation to specific destinations. Not all meditations have been made for the greater good; some may have been made with bad intentions, so be selective of what you are listening to and turn it off if it does not feel right.

6. Self-Love and Acceptance

Nurture a deep appreciation for yourself. Forgive past hurts, learn from mistakes, and cultivate self-love. Embrace the beauty of your journey, wrinkles, grey hairs, and all.

I am unsure where it started, but I didn't like who I was for quite some time. I don't think it started from childhood. I was shy growing up, but I am pretty sure I liked who I was. I had a kind heart, and my body, whilst it wasn't model-worthy, was still very beautiful. Maybe it started when I got unwell, had memory loss and didn't know myself or who I was for some time; perhaps it was when I put on weight from the medication that the doctors gave me; maybe it was when my husband and friends abandoned me when I needed them the most; or perhaps it was guilt that I was not able to protect the kids at work, even though it should not have been my guilt. I did the best I could do at the time and I was ordered to step down from the case.

I didn't even realise I felt this way about myself until I became an artist and attempted to study art therapy. There were a few occasions when I was tasked to either draw myself, paint myself or make a lino print portrait of myself; wow, did I find it challenging and wow did I try to avoid it. And I did. It wasn't until I reflected on a happy moment in my childhood that I drew myself as a child with my ma (grandmother) at her house. I started crying as I realised I had finally managed to draw myself. It may have been as a child; however, it seemed to make a switch in my brain to realise that I am ok, a good person, and worthy. Even though I am older and have a few grey hairs and certainly more love handles and wrinkles, I have never been more comfortable with how I look and who I am. It is a fantastic feeling when you can love and accept yourself the way you are, a work in progress, being perfectly imperfect – or is it imperfectly perfect?

Learn to grow from your mistakes and the mistakes of others, and love yourself for who you are. Remember, you are beautiful and capable of great things. You can fill your heart with love for yourself and others and do the things that support you to become the best version of yourself, or you can choose to do the opposite. Faith or fear, it's your choice!

THE 12-POINT SURVIVAL PLAN

7. Connect with Nature

Incorporate nature into your daily routine. Whether it's a backyard stroll, beachside contemplation, or mountain retreat, let the healing power of nature be a constant presence in your life.

Connecting with nature is something we could all do with more of in our lives; however, some of us need it more than others, especially those suffering from depression, anxiety, PTSD, brain trauma or memory loss. Today, we live in such an unnatural, busy world full of artificial noise, lighting, chemicals and material; there are all sorts of frequencies buzzing about from electrical devices, WiFi, mobile phones, and so many other things, and it can all become a bit overwhelming. I hate spending too much time in shopping centres with artificial lights and no fresh air, and I can get overwhelmed by all the noise, the crying and screaming kids, and the loud noises of the coffee machines. There was a time when I couldn't go there at all, but I am better at it now. Still, give me the choice of whether to go shopping or go for a walk, swim, paint or draw outside, and I will choose all of them over shopping any day.

I am fortunate that I picked up on the fact that I would feel better and could heal when I was in nature. I was undoubtedly on the right track with this, as many studies have shown the healing effect of being in nature. Do your research, and you will be amazed by what you find. Interestingly, I have found my children and other family members are the same when spending time in nature, and they have realised how much it benefits them and realise now that they need to make time for it.

I look back at my children's lives; they are keen surfers and love getting into the ocean. There was a period in their lives when the lifestyle of being a teenager and young adult kept them away from the surf for a while, and I could see the change in them when this was happening, I could also see the change for the better when they realised it was missing from their lives, and they started including a dip in the ocean and a surf more often. They are certainly much happier and healthier for doing so.

Nature and sunshine have been vital to my healing and recovery. Make sure you schedule some into your day. It could be as simple as spending time in your backyard, walking around your garden, gardening, or just sitting there and relaxing. It could be getting out into the bush or going along the beach, the mountains, or the river. It could even be going into the water for a swim or snorkelling underneath the sea to see all the fish and marine life. Wherever it ends up being, you will know the places where you feel at home and feel like you belong. If I go too long without sunshine, I can feel my mood slipping backwards. There have been a few occasions when it has rained for weeks that I have pulled out a very bright light that is like daylight and sat near it. It is not the same, but it is definitely worth using when times get desperate, and mother nature is not giving you what is needed.

8. Cold Showers for a Boost

Explore the stimulating benefits of cold showers. Challenge yourself to embrace the cold, discovering its positive impact on your mood and overall well-being.

Now, please stick with me on this one. It can seem overwhelming, but it certainly makes you feel better. Each day, I try to spend a little bit of time under the cold running water at the end of my shower. Alternatively, I go for a swim, which is just as good, maybe even a little better, as I get the healing power of submerging myself in the salt water. If you don't believe me, try it! I even do this in winter. Let me give you a heads-up: not all cold water is equal. I live on the coast and have travelled inland occasionally. The shock of the cold water initially hitting me caused me to squeal out loud unexpectedly on a few occasions as the water was way colder than it was at home.

9. Humour as a Coping Mechanism

Infuse humour into your life, seeking joy in laughter. Embrace the lighter side of challenges, turning to comedies or jokes to lift your spirits during challenging days.

A little humour is known to beat the blues. I now take life a little lighter and see the funny side of many things. Not everyone gets my humour, but that's ok; I do, and that's the main thing. This helps me stay in a good place. I often make a funny cartoon in my imagination; it helps me smile when life is complicated. I might put on a good comedy or read some jokes if I have a bad day. I have a friend on Facebook who usually posts a joke daily. I look forward to reading his daily posts; they make me smile.

10. Acts of Kindness

Despite personal struggles, extend kindness to others. Simple gestures, like a phone call or a smile, can brighten someone else's day and bring warmth to your own. This may seem overwhelming, especially for people who need help themselves. How can you help anybody else when you are not getting the help you need? I understand. It can be challenging. However, I found doing something simple to brighten somebody else's day or helping another person made them feel better and in turn brightened my day.

It could be as simple as a phone call to tell somebody they're not alone or encouraging them. It could be as simple as smiling at somebody, opening a door, giving them a lift, or helping them with a task. There are so many things that you can do to brighten somebody's day, even when you are suffering yourself.

THE 12-POINT SURVIVAL PLAN

11. Community and Communication

Foster a sense of community and open communication. Whether within your family or a wider community, the support network you build can be a powerful antidote to challenges.

It is a fact there are a few areas in the world that have the happiest, longest-living people. These areas are called 'Blue Zones'. There's one thing that they all have in common: a sense of community and coming together. They have families and communities that love and support each other. They have little or no depression and many illnesses they are immune to, and if healing needs to happen, it happens way quicker because they feel loved and supported. I have seen many people in families and communities bury their heads in the sand, saying, "It's not my problem", and they look out just for themselves.

I have seen families broken because of ego and because they won't take the time to communicate. And often, they would find that with communication, they would recognise there is no reason to fight or argue. With the simple act of communication, they would understand how each other is feeling, often finding out that it's either been a miscommunication or that the other person has not entirely had the chance to understand a person's situation and that there's really no reason to fight.

Sometimes, it's taken out of our hands, and you may not have the supportive family you need, or there is that friend, neighbour, or family member who won't try to communicate and make peace. Make the best of the situation and find love and support from the other parts of your community. It might be through friends or those in your church, family, or some other community you are involved with. If you see someone isolated, struggling, and without family support, offer them some kindness and support, and I am sure they will be forever grateful. I have some dear friends who are like sisters, friends who, after my mum and dad passed away and knowing I was going to be on my own for a big part of Christmas day, welcomed me into their family and their home to celebrate Christmas with them. This act of kindness means the world to me.

12. Spirituality and Inner Connection

Delve into your spiritual side, exploring the profound connections that transcend the material realm. This aspect deserves a deeper discussion, one I'm eager to explore with you in a later chapter.

My connection to God has been essential to my healing and survival, so much so that I have a chapter dedicated to it later in this book.

THE 12-POINT SURVIVAL PLAN

PEARLS OF WISDOM:

Faith or fear, the choice is yours!

Kind words are like honey – sweet to the soul and healthy for the body (Proverbs 16:24)

Chapter 6

THINKING OUTSIDE THE SQUARE WITH MY RECOVERY

I tried so many things to try to get better. I went to counselling, and I tried medication. I tried something called EFT, which involved reliving a trauma by talking about the event and then tapping at the same time in different parts of your body. I even tried electric shock treatment, but nothing seemed to work. The counselling and the tapping seemed to reinforce how bad life had gotten. It was a reminder every time of how ****** life was, and to tell you the truth, it just depressed me even more and reminded me of how much of a****** I was. Initially, it was OK to talk about what happened, and I needed to do it, but I didn't need to review the same stuff repeatedly. I needed to break my state and find new ways of coping. My 12-point survival plan helped me; however, I also needed to challenge myself, confront my demons and move forward with my life.

While trying to get better through doctors and counselling, the doctor told me that a good form of treatment was exposure therapy. It seemed pretty scary, as even talking about the incident in counselling would trigger me and send me backwards. I honestly thought exposure therapy would not work, and at the time, I was a single mother responsible for two young children; there was no way in the world I was going to be set backwards and get worse.

As my children got older and I spread my wings a little more, I began to realise how much my trauma was holding me back. I was missing out on life. I had started dating a wonderful man – he was a bit of a workaholic, but he was still very special to me. He worked full-time in a job requiring a lot of his time and attention and was also a single dad. He also had a love for the country, and every weekend, he would go and work on his farm. To spend time with him, I would have to go away with him every second weekend and spend time with him on his farm. You would think this would have been a wonderful experience, considering I had grown up on a farm myself, and it was one of my fondest childhood memories. Unfortunately, it was not that way in the beginning, as it triggered my post-traumatic stress.

To get to the property, we would drive for hours, aggravating my already challenged back and neck. We often arrived at night and drove down a long dirt track, and the headlights would eerily illuminate a long line of trees surrounding both sides of the dirt track. The scene would bring back memories of an incident during my policing career. Those memories, upon arrival, were not a good start to the trip.

My partner was also a keen shooter and hunter. On each trip, he would shoot on his property. He took me shooting with him for the first time, and I held the spotlight. The sound of the gun firing would echo and send chills all through my body and mind; it felt dreadful. I could feel the sadness and trauma from the animal that he had shot, and the feeling would stay with me for days. I tried to be tough and not show any emotion. I didn't want my boyfriend to see me as a mess, so I put on my mask of bravado and pretended I was OK. I certainly wasn't.

Even though I would stay at the house instead of going shooting on the following trips, he would still go. From the house, I could hear the gunfire sending chills and panic through my body. After some time, it all got too much for me, and I stopped going to the farm, which made it very hard for us to have time for each other. I was also missing out on things at home, as I had become afraid of the dark and wouldn't go out at night to be social if I was on my own. The restrictions that were happening due to my post-traumatic stress seemed to be making my depression worse. I was not going to let this beat me.

I investigated where my closest pistol range was. I was not going to let the sound of a gun firing on a farm ruin my life again. They had an open day when people could go and try pistol shooting to see if they wanted to join. I signed up. When I got there, I had panic running through my body. For a while, I just sat there and couldn't move. I imagined God standing beside me and holding my hand as I left the car.

Eventually, I mustered up the courage to go in, introduced myself, did a quick theory test, and then off to the range it was. It was the first time I had held a gun since leaving the job. It felt weird. The targets were all put up, and I was ready to shoot. Wow, the emotions running through me at the time were beyond words. I stood there with my gun pointing down range and pulled the trigger, bang, bang, bang. The sound of many guns firing at once echoed and vibrated through my entire body. Once again, words could not describe this feeling. The tears welled in my eyes, and I held my breath for a bit. We went down the range to examine my target, and the instructor was quite impressed with how I did. He commented on how good my shooting was. I managed to get all the bullets on target, most of which were close to the centre. I smiled and had a slight feeling of pride and said to myself, "You go, girl, you've still got it".

After finishing my pistol shooting, I spoke to the instructor and told him that I was an ex-police officer and that I had come along to shoot to help with my PTSD. He was very kind and organised another instructor to take me under her wing. I returned to the pistol range several times to shoot with the instructors. These two beautiful souls have no idea how much their kindness and time really meant to me. Shooting at the range challenged me, improved my confidence, and helped me move forward.

I finally felt ready to return to the farm. When I did, I enjoyed my time there. I walked through the bushland and rode the quad up the mountain. I watched the cattle, horses, birds, and dogs. It looked so beautiful, watching the sun break through the fog and the trees as it tried to reach the sky. I finally felt the peace I had found as a child growing up on the farm. I did hear gunfire again, and I was OK, and I couldn't wait to return. Sadly, too much time had passed, with us not being together and me not going to the farm, and the relationship ended. I wish I had been able to communicate better at the time to let him know how much I cared for him and how hard I had worked so we could be together. It was so sad that my post-traumatic stress and past trauma had prevented me from being with somebody that I loved and in a place that I loved. After all that hard work I had put in and my relationship ending, I slipped backwards. That was OK. I became aware of this, and I was determined that there was no way in the world that I was going to let my post-traumatic stress ruin my life again.

I had always loved camping and realised that I had not done it since my marriage had ended. Here I was, a single woman with post-traumatic stress, and I wanted to give it a go again. I got a tent and tried camping with my sister and her husband. I found it hard to put the tent up with a bad back. I also didn't sleep a wink, as I was so on guard the whole night; after all, the tent didn't lock, and I needed a locked door to feel safe. I loved the trip but hated the days that followed, as my depression was awful due to not getting any sleep the night before. Sleep is essential for me to keep my depression under control.

I wanted to keep camping, but I knew I couldn't do it the traditional way of sleeping in a tent, so I converted my Suzuki 4-wheel drive by taking the back seats out and putting a plank of wood in the back allowing the floor to be flat. I put in a fridge and a mattress and went away for a few nights. It felt good to be out in nature again, and I loved my freedom. However, the little four-wheel-drive Suzuki felt a little cramped.

My mum and dad died within three months of each other, and my dad passed away on my birthday of all days. Not long after my parents passing my sister and brother retreated into their own worlds due to their grief. My kids were at an age where they were busy living their own lives and hanging out with friends and possibly doing their own grieving. I felt so alone and sad and my depression was becoming worse. I needed another solution – there was no way I was going to let the depression get on top of me again. So I thought outside the square and bought myself a big Mercedes Sprinter van, which was converted into a camper van. I thought it was terrific; it had an internal kitchen, toilet, and shower. I could lock it up when I slept and stand up in it. I thought all my Christmases had come at once. I thought I could rent my house out, camp, have adventures, reduce my stress and the responsibilities of running a house and that it would help with the financial pressures I was feeling at the time.

I felt a sense of happiness once more, but this happiness quickly turned into sadness and stress. Even though it was a brand-new van, it leaked continuously for 18 months. I took it back to the company about ten times; each time, they would have it for anywhere from one month to three months. Towards the end, they became rude to me because I was a single woman, and they refused to help or listen to me, telling me that they had fixed the problem and for me to go and stop wasting their time.

I took the van away, and when it was raining I recorded the footage of the rain pouring into the van and took my complaint to Consumer Affairs. I can now understand how the caravan company got the nickname Junko. They now had no choice but to fix the leak, but by then, the whole thing had caused so much stress on me, and we had been in lockdowns from COVID-19 for lengthy periods that I just wanted to let the van go. I felt so sad.

After a while, I tried to look for another van but found it impossible due to all the COVID restrictions and the lack of supplies coming into the country. I managed to get a Toyota Hiace van, and I got a company to set it up as a camper. I like it; however, I miss having a bathroom and kitchen inside the van. The positives are that it fits in my garage and makes a great everyday vehicle as it only takes up a single car park. I have some chairs, supplies, art supplies and my fridge in the van permanently. It is excellent and very convenient; I can go out and do some drawing or painting, spend time in nature, quickly make myself a cuppa, or have lunch.

I may change my camper or vehicle down the track, but I am grateful for it now and love the flexibility and adventures it brings. It certainly helps with my post-traumatic stress and depression. The main thing about camping is knowing that I am safe, sleeping in a vehicle where I can lock the doors and enjoy life while still having the camping experience. I have met some beautiful people

THINKING OUTSIDE THE SQUARE WITH MY RECOVERY

whilst I have been camping. They invited me on a few of their camping trips. I have enjoyed their friendship, and I am grateful as they made me feel more comfortable with camping, which has been very helpful in my recovery.

I still feared being in the dark, especially on my own. Sometimes, this fear prevented me from going out with friends in the evening as I didn't want to walk back to my car alone in the dark. A few things that have helped with this are ideas that would certainly be considered as thinking outside the square. I can remember my doctor telling me the story of a war veteran, and when he was having flashbacks, he would imagine many Dalmatian dogs in the situation instead. I tried it, but it didn't work for me. He also said that exposure therapy can help. The idea terrified me because often, when I spoke of incidences with my counsellor, it would send me backwards. Eventually, the two ideas got me thinking: what if I could combine all these things but change the environment and my mindset to help me when I felt uncomfortable? I did just that.

There were two out-of-the-box ideas that helped me feel more comfortable in the dark. The first was being naked, which I know may sound weird to few of you. I had the opportunity to be on a property late at night, and I had the chance to be naked and feel safe. There is a saying when you're about to go on stage or do public speaking, and you feel nervous or overwhelmed, you should imagine your audience naked to break your state and let go of your fear. Being on a property surrounded by bushland in the dark, stripped back bare and naked, precisely the way that God had me enter this world, did the same thing for me. It managed to break my fear and helped me feel more at ease with bushland and darkness. Standing there naked, feeling vulnerable in a different way, I could feel the cool breeze gently touching and caressing every part of my body. The sensation felt beautiful and freeing, and it was a feeling that I had never felt before. This experience was able to break my state of fear and helped me to accept and feel more comfortable with darkness.

After that experience, I was able to challenge myself a little more. I had an exciting adventure on the lake on a boat overnight. Being on a small boat with no lights, surrounded by vast amounts of water, and with no locked door was very eerie and scary. I felt very vulnerable, but I was in good company and felt safe despite being scared. The person I went on the adventure with had no idea how much I was being challenged that night and how scared I was. Once again, that mask of bravado was on. I am very grateful to that person and the adventure I shared with him, as it certainly helped with my recovery.

To get through, I concentrated on my breathing and the sounds of the water hitting against the side of the boat. I watched the way that the full moonlight reflected on

THINKING OUTSIDE THE SQUARE WITH MY RECOVERY

the water and the shadows and the highlights that the moonlight made when it hit the ripples in the water. I breathed in and smelt the cool, salty, fishy air so I could remain calm. The fishing, chatting, and drawing on my iPad were also a nice distraction. I didn't manage to sleep a wink that night, and I returned to the shores dirty, smelly, salty, tired and grumpy the next day, but I also felt invigorated and so glad I made the trip and pushed myself outside of my comfort zone and the safety of my home. Being absorbed by the darkness all night helped me become more comfortable with darkness and night-time.

So, in a way, the doctor was right: exposure therapy does work. I just needed to think outside the square and take opportunities to put my unique spin on it so that it suited me and my needs. I changed it to something that was the same but different so that it did not trigger my trauma to send me backward again.

Another creative technique that I used along my journey is visualisation. When I was learning to meditate, one of the meditations was going to my happy place. The farm I grew up on as a child was one of those places. I would take myself there in my imagination when I needed to find some calm, when the sounds of sirens would trigger panic, or when I drove past a motor vehicle accident. Upon hearing the sirens, I would freeze and start feeling depressed. Some days, this would prevent me from doing things. When I listened to the siren or saw an accident,

I would start crying uncontrollably, and I would stop what I was doing and return home.

Meditation has become handy in this situation. I can quickly close my eyes and imagine myself at my childhood farm, sitting on the river bank, looking over the river, listening to the sound the bridge made when a car drove over it (clackety clack), feeling the cool breeze touching my face and even the smell of fresh cow paddies which undoubtedly made it feel like I was there and also made me laugh. Sometimes, I imagine a light of protection surrounding me, or I will have a conversation with God and imagine myself lovingly handing over the thing or person that was troubling me. I would feel calmer and more at peace once I had handed my burdens to Him.

Another technique I find helpful is something like what a bird or a dog might do after a stressful situation: physically shaking it off. This one can be tricky when surrounded by people as they may think you are acting a little strange, so I would usually take myself somewhere private and physically shake off the bad energy or bad thoughts. Sometimes, if I am feeling a little small or lacking confidence or fearing an event, I will bend down and make myself small and slowly bring myself up, making myself tall, reaching for the sky, and making a roaring sound like a lion. This technique helps me feel stronger and more confident and is best done privately.

THINKING OUTSIDE THE SQUARE WITH MY RECOVERY

Another outside-the-square solution has been the discovery of rose-coloured glasses. Life really is better looking at life through rose-coloured glasses. Who would have thought that a saying I had heard throughout life could also be true for me? My hard work to improve my memory loss and cognition has helped. However, I sometimes struggled to sit and concentrate on tasks for long periods, and I found doing paperwork challenging. Sometimes, I would take a micro-dose of Ritalin to help me. However, this can have side effects. I found an optometrist who specialised in tinted neurology glasses, and we found that I responded best to having a slight red tinge in my glasses. Having a slight red tinge in my glasses helps me concentrate better when reading lengthy documents and books, and it also helps me when doing paperwork and assignments. The glasses somehow seem to make life a little better all around.

I am very sensitive to medications; a lot of them have made my life worse or have nearly killed me, so I've had to think outside the square here, too. Most of the time, I choose not to take any medication, but on those days that are just too much or when I am in too much pain, I have a little extra help. It was good that I had a doctor who listened to me and was also open to new ideas, as many of the medications were not mainstream for treating my condition.

I found that micro-dosing for short periods is the best option for me. When my pain is at a level that I can't handle, and Panadol doesn't help, I will use medicinal cannabis oil that is applied to the skin of the painful area. Using the oil this way does not give me any side effects; there is no high feeling, it does not change my brain functioning, and it's not absorbed into my bloodstream. I also find micro-dosing for one or two days with LA Ritalin helpful when my emotions become too out of balance; taking it for more extended periods does not work due to the side effects. These things all help me, but I still have to work hard and utilise my 12-point recovery plan.

It would be good if more doctors could think outside the box when treating their patients. If you or a loved one is struggling and cannot find help or a solution through mainstream treatments, I encourage you to get creative about your recovery, think outside the square and find something that works for you. Don't give up!

PEARLS OF WISDOM:

*If you can dream it, you can make it happen!
(Unknown)*

Life is too short to dress sad! (Unknown)

*Those who trust in the Lord will find new strength.
They will soar high on wings like eagles. (Isaiah 40:31)*

Chapter 7

FINDING THE MISSING PIECE IN THE PUZZLE

Part of my journey of healing was learning life coaching. Here, I discovered some missing pieces in the puzzle of my life. I discovered some necessities we all need to include in our lives, which can be the difference between achieving great things and our lives being balanced and content or our lives being out of balance and dysfunctional (Wow, how did I not know this? Was someone hiding this piece of the puzzle?).

These necessities included security and certainty, variety and adventures, a feeling of importance and worth, love and belonging, growth and improvement, and making a difference and contributing. While all of these are necessary for a good life, as individuals, we will gravitate to some more than others, giving them more importance; this can vary with each person. When I discovered this, I realised my life had become unbalanced as I didn't have any of these things. It is interesting, though, as the bible also touches on many of these points.

Yeah, there were reasons for this; my PTSD, depression and chronic pain had caused me to lose my job, my family, my friends, my memory, my home, and the secure income I had. All my security and certainty had been thrown out the window. I certainly had no variety or adventures. I was in survival mode and had two children dependent on me, and I could hardly look after myself; there was no time for variety. I had to learn all the basics again to be a mum and learn how to take care of myself and my children.

As for feeling important and significant, what was that? I had memory loss, I had lost my job, and I had lost my family. All the things that I thought gave me a sense of importance in the world because they allowed me to help others and feel like I was needed and had a purpose were gone.

Love and connections – I certainly didn't feel these. My husband had walked away from me, I only had my children half the time because we had shared custody, and my family and friends didn't understand my PTSD and depression, so I didn't feel like I belonged or connected anywhere.

Growth and improvement – I certainly didn't feel like I was growing and improving. Instead, I felt like I was shrinking; I had had memory loss, and I was having to learn all the basics again. And making a difference and contributing; once again, I was in survival mode. There was no time for me to be able to contribute to anything or anyone, or so I thought.

When I look back on this, I realise now how I was feeling so unbalanced and so unhappy and how life was feeling so dysfunctional. I learned that things needed to change if it was going to get better. I also realised that I had limitations. I had challenges that other people didn't have, and I had two children who were my responsibility. I needed to make sure they were OK. I was also aware that working on all these things simultaneously was impossible due to my circumstances, and that everyone ranks their life's necessities differently. So, I started to work on the ones that I could work on and thought were more important to me and my children, and then I slowly worked on the others so I could feel more balance and peace in my life. Remember, everyone is different here, and we all find different ways to fill these needs; it's a matter of reflecting and asking yourself if this is a healthy or unhealthy way to achieve this need. For me, these are some of the things that helped.

1. Security and Certainty

I purchased a home where I could feel safe and secure, and it felt like home. I got this wrong initially; I thought the most important thing was a beautiful view. I am an artist and can be attracted to beautiful things. I realised that this home wasn't the be-all and end-all; I didn't feel safe in it. This was important for me, since I was suffering from PTSD. So, I decided to sell the house and move to a more secure and healing place.

I established some routines. To start, this was mainly based on my kids. They were the ones who needed to be at school, play their sport and be fed and loved. Once I got this down pat, I could look at creating this for myself. I organised to learn some basic meals to make life a little easier, so that I didn't have to think about unnecessary things and I could concentrate on the essential things. I also made sure that I kept a diary and a list of things that needed to be done. This certainty helped and being organised allowed me to function better.

After I got the basics down pat, I could concentrate on other things. I enrolled in some courses to learn and get my brain functioning again. I knew this would be hard to do on my own. I couldn't get any other professional help as the insurance company would only help me if I got a work certificate saying I could return to work. (They had to be kidding; I was struggling to stay alive, function and run a house, and they wanted me to go back to work full-time before they would give me any help. They were cruel, they were barbaric.) Enrolling in courses gave me certainty, gave me routine, and pushed me to show up and do. I had the benefit of some help from the tutors.

If you support a friend or family, think outside the square to work out ways to bring security and certainty back into their life. It can be simple things. Even having them know that you are a constant in their life, you have their back, and they are loved can be a form of security and certainty.

2. Variety and Adventures

For someone who is suffering from anxiety, depression or PTSD, variety and adventures can be a challenge, but for others, it just comes naturally, and they thrive on it.

For me, I just started with some little things, some things that pushed me outside of my comfort zone but that I felt safe doing. I started leaving the house more, exercising, meeting new people, exploring my hometown, studying, and trying new foods. I started concentrating on my art and learning new things. As time passed, I started researching further. I did several overseas trips. My first was to Bali, and later I went to Hawaii. I had done some travel before I got unwell, but I had stopped as it felt safer in my own home.

I later purchased a van to do some camping trips, as I felt safer being able to lock the doors and sleep in my van rather than camp in a tent where I felt vulnerable. Whilst I have not done any huge exploring overseas like others may have, these short trips have given me variety, confidence, and adventures and, indeed, put a smile on my face. As a bonus, I have met some beautiful people along the way.

If you support a loved one or a friend on their recovery journey, you could ask them out for lunch, exercise, a movie, a show, or a little adventure; remember, some people may need to start small. Lunch could be a picnic, somewhere in nature, somewhere quiet, somewhere they feel safe away from the noise and the hustle and bustle.

3. Importance and Worth

This can be a tricky one for somebody who has a lot of healing to do, for example someone who has endured memory loss, loss of family and friends and loss of their occupation. It certainly was for me; I had lost my identity and didn't feel significant or important at all. I would look around at others and see that they had things in their lives that mattered. They had their careers, loved ones, friends, and hobbies and contributed to church or local sports. I had nothing. This wasn't always the case before I was unwell; I had a family, I had lots of friends, I had a career, I was strong, I was fit, I would exercise, and I would play sports with a team. I would contribute to my community and in turn felt significant.

I started concentrating on the most important thing to me: my children. I had previously worked with young offenders, kids at risk, and children with challenging lives, and because of that, I realised I needed to be the best mum I could be. To do that, I needed to get my memory back, be well, be present, and be there for them. To protect them and teach them. Doing that gave me a purpose, importance and significance. Not as much as I had before and not as much as others had, but at least it was something.

It wasn't until later in life that I realised just how critical this need is. My kids were all grown up; they had their own lives now. My mum and dad were very ill for many years, and I had to be there for them and help to take care of them. When they passed, I also lost my brother and sister for a while, as they had become so overwhelmed with grief that they had lost their way and, in turn, had lost communication with me. Life was so unfair; it seemed to be one arduous journey after another. Was life ever going to give me a break? Life, people, and the world all seemed cruel, unfair, and so hard I was nearly ready to give up.

It was here I realised that I couldn't; if I left this world, I would be leaving my kids and, in time, my grandkids, in a cruel and unfair world. How could I do this to them? How could I show them that it is okay to give up? How could I cause heartache for the person who found me or the emergency service workers who would have to come? I COULD NOT! Things had to change, and I had to make the world a better place, not just for me but for my children and the generations to come.

I know I can't instantly change the world and that I am no superhero. However, I decided there were small steps I could take to make this world a better place and hoped that each small ripple would create another ripple until enough ripples made a wave.

I tried, and even when I was feeling down, I challenged myself to perform small acts of kindness. Some days, it was as simple as a smile at a stranger, friend or loved one or a hug. It may have been complimenting what someone was wearing, how they looked, their beautiful smile, or the excellent service they gave. It may have been an act of kindness, like opening a door for someone or helping someone in need by providing a meal or dropping off a care package. I hoped the person receiving this would benefit from my acts of kindness and pass it on.

I decided to share my journey with others. If I could make someone else's journey a little easier or give them some hope to keep living and keep going, then it was worth every minute to live a long life myself.

FINDING THE MISSING PIECE IN THE PUZZLE

I decided to acknowledge that I am an artist. For a long time, I felt insignificant as people would ask me what I do for work, and I couldn't give them an answer as I didn't believe in myself, I didn't think art was an occupation (I was wrong). I now realise I am significant, and I can say I am a mother, a sister, an aunt, an artist, a manager, an investor, a mentor and teacher, and a child of God. I am me, and I am okay.

Reflecting on life, the previous work I did and some behaviours I saw in others, I would see people trying to make themselves feel good in unhealthy ways like alcohol and drug abuse, causing and engaging in arguments, running others down or hanging out with people that they viewed as less skilled or not as good as themselves. If you see this as an area where you or a loved one needs to improve, try to take a healthier and more balanced approach, challenge yourself, and channel your competitive nature into learning a new hobby or skill. Work towards becoming an expert in your craft or profession. Be kind to yourself and acknowledge how far you have come, the skills you have attained, and how you can pass on this knowledge or make this world a better place. Remember, it can be as simple as teaching and being there for your kids or giving a stranger a smile or a compliment.

4. Love and Belonging

Love and belonging can get more challenging as we get older. When we are born, it comes more naturally to us, but over time, this can become more of a challenge as we have built up memories of how others have hurt us. This can leave us with a feeling that we need to protect ourselves, so we put walls up, and some may have even shut people out. This is quite unhealthy for us. As humans, we have been designed to need love, connection and a sense of belonging. This is not a new concept; it has been mentioned many times throughout history in the study of the 'Blue Zones', which are the countries where people live the longest and are the happiest. They all have something in common: they have a culture of love and connection and communities and families supporting each other. Well-known neurologist Sigmund Freud discovered it in his research, and it can even be found many times in the bible: love our God, love our neighbours.

The few countries in the Blue Zone know the importance of this and put it into practice in their communities, and they reap the rewards. Unfortunately, many countries have lost this skill, or they have yet to be taught the importance of it, and sadly, they pay the price for it, with increased sickness and illness and depression and anxiety in their communities and families.

FINDING THE MISSING PIECE IN THE PUZZLE

It seems that the importance of family and friends has deteriorated with time. It is so easy to get a divorce these days and walk away from a family, throw away friendships that have lasted decades for something trivial that happened, something as simple as somebody making a decision not to get a vaccine. It appears that we live in a throwaway society, not just with material items but also with relationships. No one wants to put the hard work in anymore; the crazy thing is it is often more complicated and challenging for the whole family when somebody chooses to walk away and break up a family for something trivial, like they're bored, thought the grass was greener on the other side, or were hunting for that next shiny thing. I have seen some families destroyed simply because someone wouldn't make an effort to communicate – if they had, they would discover that they had misread the situation – while in other cases someone would not forgive a mistake that was not even intentional (we are all human and are bound to make mistakes from time to time).

Don't get me wrong; I have certainly seen situations where, for the safety of a partner or children, a marriage or relationship needed to end. But I have also seen marriages end and children and partners suffering consequently for something trivial that could have been sorted out with communication and love. At work, I have even seen someone wanting their partner arrested and charged for breaching an AVO just because their partner farted; we certainly need more love and communication in families.

While love, belonging and connection are essential, and for some, they might be at the top of their list, it is necessary to remember to also look after yourself, nurture yourself, and love yourself. Don't put yourself in a position where you feel unsafe or feel mentally or physically abused, or you are craving love and jumping from one sexual partner to another regularly and having unhealthy relationships (sex does not equal love). Love and connecting can come from your family, friends and our communities; it is about connecting and looking out for one another. It could be as simple as taking a meal to somebody who is in need, it may be doing a job for somebody else who is struggling and can't do it themselves, it could just be a simple phone call asking are you OK or it could be a warm embrace hello to a friend or family so that they feel like you care.

I can remember one stage of my life where I felt so alone. I felt like there was nobody, no love, and no connection or sense of belonging. I was so unwell at that stage of my life, and I was also hurt by the ones that I loved; I was so broken that I could not forge any new relationships, and I just wanted to lock myself away from the world. At that time, I was extremely blessed by a woman who had come into my life, the mother of one of my son's friends. That beautiful woman invited me to her church, where

I discovered Christ. From then on, when I was feeling alone and sad and felt like I had nobody, I imagined God there with me, loving and supporting me. I no longer felt alone. From there, I ventured out and connected with others more and more and even managed to find love.

5. Growth and Improvement

I also worked out that I needed growth and improvement. We can all benefit from these things, but ensuring you do it correctly is vital. I've seen some families and children neglected by parents who had this at the top of their list. They had no time for their family, and other parts of their lives were neglected so that they could be the best or at the top of their field or just because they want to feel that sense of achievement continually. At the end of their lives, they feel like they have missed something and have made no time to forge connections with others, or they may wonder why their kids have gone off the rails. Growth can happen in many ways; sometimes, it means getting a certificate or degree. However, we can grow and learn in other ways too, whether learning a new way to communicate or a new recipe, hobby, or exercise. Some may grow spiritually or personally.

With everything I went through, growth became something important in my life. However, I also had to learn grace and patience. I was a perfectionist and had done alright in life. I had studied and got qualifications, had what I thought was a perfect family and friends, had a home, a good job, or so I thought at that time. Life was sweet until PTSD, but then so many things changed. It was so hard to accept where I was. I was looking at all those who were getting ahead, and I seemed to have gone backwards. I had to take my time to recover and work out my priorities as my kids needed me also; they came first. However, I would learn things daily and exercise regularly to become a better mum and a better me. To strengthen my brain and my body. I had to learn not to compare myself to others and where they were in their lives, as that just made me more depressed. Instead, I learned to compare myself to myself and make continual minor improvements each day. The Japanese call this Kaizen: change for the better or continual improvement. Life started improving after that.

6. Making a Difference and Contributing

This can be a tricky one for someone struggling with chronic pain, depression, anxiety, memory loss or other health challenges. It is so easy to get consumed in the survival mentality, only thinking about looking after myself and my children. If I can hardly do that, how can I help anyone else? Hey, I get it – what do they tell you if the plane is going down? Put your oxygen mask on first, and then help someone else. You can't help anyone if you pass out. The same goes for life. Sometimes, we must take the necessary time to ensure we are okay. I

FINDING THE MISSING PIECE IN THE PUZZLE

learned after a while that I couldn't just concentrate on myself and my needs, as it did not allow me to be happy, content, or find peace.

I also realised that I now had limitations. I could no longer contribute in ways that I used to, like volunteering at a nursing home or doing volunteer first aid at events. I could no longer protect the community as a police officer as I had done previously. This made me angry and depressed for a while, but then I had a light bulb moment. I realised that there were things I could do to improve this world.

I reflected for a bit and observed others. My aunt was a huge influence, and that was where the change started. She is one of the happiest and most positive people I know and is living a long and healthy life. When she retired and was widowed, she didn't just stop. She was always busy, had interests and hobbies, volunteered, and helped others. I used to joke with her that I had to book a time slot in her calendar to catch up as she had something scheduled every minute of every day. Even now, in her mid-80s, she constantly checks in on her family and friends and sends them pearls of wisdom and encouragement; that is her contribution. My GP doctor is another person I have looked at who is healthy and happy. He is also in his mid-80s and still working and contributing to others. He says that he will work until the day he dies. I thought maybe there was something in this.

I started thinking of others more and working out ways to contribute using the abilities that I have, given my individual challenges. I started doing the same as my aunty; I would check in on my friends and family who needed extra encouragement, love and support. I started contributing a little more to my local art community, helping to keep the place going and helping at community events, and I am now the welcoming party at church. I have accepted that I contribute to this world through my art, writing, and giving a warm smile or acts of kindness. I encourage others to do the same and find some way they can contribute to their community, family or friends. Kindness is contagious; if everyone demonstrates it, the world will be a better place in no time. The most exciting thing about contributing is that you can fulfil all the other needs in one act.

FINDING THE MISSING PIECE IN THE PUZZLE

PEARLS OF WISDOM:

To survive and thrive, I need to change, adapt, think outside the square, keep moving, growing, learning, and contributing, and keep the love and kindness flowing.

(Sharran Makin)

The best feeling in the world is to be able to help someone else other than yourself. (Charmaine J. Forde)

God is not unjust: he will not forget your work and the love you have shown him as you have helped his people and continue to help them. We want each of you to show the same diligence to the very end so that what you hope for may be fully realised. (Hebrews 6:10-11)

Chapter 8

THE POWER OF NEUROPLASTICITY

Who would have guessed that the brain can change? For quite some time, I had no memories at all, so you can imagine how excited I was when I discovered neuroplasticity and the power of meditation. Whilst I could talk, I can remember finding it quite challenging to converse with people. In the beginning, sometimes mid-sentence, I couldn't find the words I wanted to come out. I would pause and try to explain things differently. Quite often, people would snap or get frustrated with me, saying, "Can you give me the short version?" I don't think they understood that I couldn't give them the short answer because I couldn't get the right words. So, I would describe things instead of using the words I needed, and they would get the extended version.

It is interesting how sometimes the right people are placed in your life for a reason. They may not stay, but their presence opens new doors and possibilities. This is how I discovered neuroplasticity and meditation. I had the opportunity to listen to a meditation by a man, Sandy McGregor. I loved the meditation, and I found it fascinating to learn about him. I started researching this man and decided to attend a workshop with him in Tasmania. I was terrified at the time as I was still having difficulties with my memory and navigating, and I had no idea how I was going to get there. I shared my fears with Sandy on the phone, and he and his beautiful wife decided that it would be best if I stayed with them the night before and travelled to Tasmania together.

I also had my mum and dad in my ear. They were worried about me too, but for different reasons; they thought that I was going there to join some cult and get brainwashed. They decided to drive me to Sydney to drop me off. They met Sandy and his wife, which eased their mind, and they felt confident and comfortable with my travels.

Whilst away on this retreat, I learned the art of meditation and some basics in neuroplasticity. I found the meditations relaxing, and being away from the pressures of home in the beautiful village of Poatina was a welcomed relief.

THE POWER OF NEUROPLASTICITY

Even though it was November, the village was freezing compared to back home. I was so glad that I packed lots of warm clothes and my umbrella, as they were certainly needed. The air was clean and fresh, and there was a calmness in the village, probably a result of the people who lived in the community. There were the most picturesque mountain ranges, with the most delightful rainbows I could see every time I looked out the window or went for a walk. I had never seen so many rainbows.

I finally had a shimmer of hope for the future for the first time since my memory loss and being left a single mum, and I knew that I had undoubtedly made the right choice to make the journey to Tasmania. I had my first childhood memory come back whilst I was meditating. My emotions ran wild, and the tears flowed with so much force that the fire brigade could have tapped into me to put out a fire. I had to leave the room so I wouldn't disturb the others while they were still meditating. This was such a wonderful thing. They were not tears of sadness but tears of joy.

I had just had my first childhood memory return. It was a memory of my family farm, and I was with a friend who would visit from Sydney and spend time with me during the school holidays; we shared such joyous times together. I finally had some hope. The more meditation and exercise I did, the more it challenged my brain and the more memories returned. At first, it was the memories that had strong emotions, so unfortunately, a lot of the yucky police stuff came back, but the good stuff also returned, like giving birth to my amazing two sons.

My journey to Tasmania was such a blessing and opened my mind to new possibilities, leading me to explore meditation and neuroplasticity even more. I did more workshops on meditation and studied life coaching, neurolinguistic programming, and neuroplasticity. I was so excited when I discovered the book *The Brain That Changes Self* by Norman Doidge; it gave me hope that my brain could also change itself, especially after reading some inspiring and positive journeys in the book. I couldn't read it all as I was still having difficulty with reading and writing, and it is a massive book, but the tiny bit that I did read gave me hope.

To think that in the past, doctors, family, and friends would have just given up on somebody after they had a stroke or brain injury. Now, however, there is undoubtedly hope as they have discovered that the brain can rewire itself. The patient may not return to how they were before their injury, but the brain can make new pathways so they can recover and live a reasonable-to-good life. I took on board what I learned and started my recovery journey.

Recovering and improving my memory has been quite a difficult, long, and winding road. However, the journey has been well worth it, and I could not imagine being where I am today and being able to parent my children without putting in all the hard work that I did. Firstly, I employed a tutor for my eldest son, and I sat in on the lessons so that I could also learn. I was continuously challenging myself by doing number and word puzzles (I cheated a fair bit in the beginning, but that was okay as it was helping me understand words and learn to solve problems, and I found that over time, I needed to cheat less and less). I studied, and looked up words in the dictionary on my phone that I didn't know, didn't know how to spell or didn't know how to pronounce. I took myself to new places and learned new skills, and despite my struggles, I didn't give up.

For those who are challenged with memory loss, whether through an injury, a stroke or illness, or maybe you are like me and suffering from the effects of medical treatment through ECT or TMS, I encourage you not to give up hope. I encourage you to put in the hard work and keep challenging your brain. It may take a while, but stick with it; things can improve.

By accident, I discovered that creating art and photography was also good for building the neurons in my brain and helping with my recovery. Before I lost my memory, I had already started creating art and taking photographs as a hobby. I had a whole room in my house set up as a studio, and I saw my work on the walls in other people's houses, which was quite inspiring. When I saw my artwork in other people's homes and complimented them, saying how beautiful it was, I could not believe it when they told me I had created it.

Determined to be able to use the supplies that I already owned and get back to producing such beautiful art once again, I decided to take lessons so I could relearn the skills that I had lost. I found the process of creating art, painting, drawing, printmaking and photography was not only healing and helped with my depression, but it also helped to get my brain functioning better. The best way I can explain it is like having a power outage at home, where I was once in a complete blackout, and no electricity came through. Art was similar to the power company repairing the grid or an electrician coming and replacing the damaged circuit breakers in the house. It was like spreading the load and not having all the cords plugged into one power board, which was overloading the circuit. It wasn't an instant fix, and it took time to get the full benefits. However, it is similar to having a brownout at home; some electricity is better than no electricity at all.

I have also discovered that functioning at my best is about balance. Creativity is very beneficial for me, but so is using both sides of my brain. If I use the left side (responsible for analysis, language, numbers, science, and reasoning) of my brain too much or if I have too much creativity using the right side, I can become out of balance and not function at my best. I have worked out that I need a perfect combination using both sides of my brain to be the best me I can be, along with exercise and meditation.

I am very grateful that I have improved so much since my memory loss. I still need to challenge myself, though, and there is certainly room for growth and improvement. I sometimes still find reading, writing and paperwork challenging (although indeed not as hard as it was ten years ago), and some memories haven't returned, especially from a specific period. I have not worked out why every time I go past an accident, it causes me to break into uncontrollable tears (I am doing better with this now). I guess maybe some memories are better not being recovered, and on a positive note, I am now making new memories each day, and life is continually getting better.

I am so grateful for today's technology. I could not imagine what life would have been like without my smartphone and computer. The maps section on my phone has got me out of many pickles and helped me find my way home on many occasions. I have utilised the dictionary on my phone regularly. I love how I can speak into the phone, and it will send a text message for me or even read it out to me (just be careful here as Siri has misheard me a few times and she hasn't entirely sent the right message through). I don't have to use these functions on my phone anywhere near as often as I once did. Still, they have certainly been a blessing, as has the spell check on my computer. Even today, my mobile phone's calendar, alarm, and notes section are well utilised. I love how they keep me on time, and I never miss bin night anymore.

I am also grateful for the clever optometrist who discovered the power of using different coloured lenses in glasses, which could help with a person's brain and learning. This has only been a recent discovery of mine, and I have found my glasses with a slight red tinge very beneficial.

Who would have thought? Just 12 years ago, due to memory loss, I couldn't read or even write my name, yet here I am, challenging myself to study for a degree in visual art and write a book about my journey, which will hopefully help and inspire many people. My advice is to never give up hope. I may not be where I want to be (remember, I lost many years of my life from illness), but through perseverance and hard work, I am in a much better place than I was years ago, and I am so grateful to be alive today and for the many blessings that I have in my life now.

THE POWER OF NEUROPLASTICITY

PEARLS OF WISDOM:

Memories remind us that nothing lasts forever. Time is precious and should not be wasted. Enjoy life, and remember, don't count the days, but make the days count. (Unknown)

Aging may cause your skin to sag, your bones to become brittle, and some may even lose their hair; however, make sure you do not lose those childlike qualities of a curious and fun mind. (Sharran Makin)

Do not conform to the pattern of this world, but be transformed by the renewing of your mind. Then you will be able to test and approve what God's will is – his good, pleasing and perfect will. (Romans 12 -2)

Chapter 9

ART AS THERAPY, THE THREE P'S

My artistic journey had such a unique start. My mum would tell me that as a small child, I would be happiest when I had my little golden books and colouring books and pencils with me. I loved art in high school and regretted being encouraged not to take it as a subject in my HSC because apparently, it would not help me with my future. Looking back now, if someone asked me my opinion on whether to take art as a subject in their HSC, even though they did not want a career in the field, I would say go for it. Everyone needs a hobby and some downtime, and art certainly helps with relaxation and getting into a flow state. Some great ideas can come to people when they are in a flow state, and art also helps with problem-solving skills.

As it turned out, doing art as a subject in my HSC would have been very beneficial to me, as after being given some other lousy career advice, I ended up not going to university. Instead, I started my own printing business, where I needed to do graphic design and create artworks for my clients for their companies. The extra years of studying art certainly would have paid off then.

While I was a police officer, I started experimenting with painting and photography as a hobby. It was evident that I had become interested in creating art before becoming unwell and losing my memory. The odd thing was that I had forgotten this. After discovering I had memory loss and returning home from the hospital, I found that I had a whole room full of art equipment and an SLR camera at my home. It was like entering a stranger's room, and I had no idea what the equipment was for or how to use it. What was even stranger was when I would go into somebody's house and compliment them on a photograph or an artwork they had on display, and I would get the answer, "Shazy or Sharran, you did that". I would reply, "No way, it is beautiful".

I investigated my home further and found many beautiful photos, paintings, and drawings that I had done, and I couldn't even remember doing any of them.

ART AS THERAPY, THE THREE P'S

I started crying. It was so frustrating not being able to remember painting such beautiful artworks. My art room intimidated me; it was in my home, but it didn't feel like it belonged to me. I had bigger fish to fry, though, and I needed to work on many other things before getting into that room. I needed to work out how to drive, run my house, look after my kids, read and write, navigate around where I lived, and so many other things.

After tackling the bigger, more important things, I eventually ventured into my Art Room. I really had no idea where to start, so I started taking a few short courses in painting and photography. I loved immersing myself in painting and photography; it seemed to help me somehow. Somehow, concentrating on creating art took me away from my pain and suffering and helped me deal with my depression and anxiety. At the end of my short course, I found myself not creating anymore, and my depression was getting on top of me again. I tried another short course and found once again that it was helpful for me. But once again, in the end, I found myself not creating as life was so chaotic that if I didn't make the time to do my art, other things would take over. I had to work out a solution, as I was still very sick, and I had so much going on with relearning stuff and with being a single mum. However, I also knew art would be vital to my recovery.

I spoke to my doctor about this. He was very supportive, encouraging me to do my art. We discussed how art therapy would be beneficial for me to participate in. He wrote a referral asking for support from my insurance company to pay for my art therapy. It was very disappointing when they knocked it back; it was the only thing that seemed to be helping me. The therapy was way too expensive for me at the time.

It is frustrating how small-minded the worker's comp system is and how unsupportive they can be. I have also found this with other things like medications, etc. They will pay for medications and therapies that don't work and won't pay for the things that actually help. How stupid is that? It would be wonderful if the workers' compensation system, health funds, and other medical systems would be more open to what is most beneficial to each individual client and patient rather than the black-and-white thinking that they have. I am sure they would discover that their clients would recover more quickly, probably have them back to work sooner, and they would help keep families intact and save lives.

Knowing that I had no support from anyone, and I also had a desire to get well and be the best mum I could be, I decided to take my health and healing into my own hands. I discovered Hunter St TAFE, an art school right in the heart of Newcastle. I knew from how unwell I was that I would be unable to keep up with their schedule. At the time, a wonderful and supportive headmaster was running the TAFE; we worked out a plan that I would

ART AS THERAPY, THE THREE P'S

complete a one-year course over three years. It was wonderful, and here, I immersed myself in creativity. It also gave me a social outlet and helped with my healing.

There was another positive to attending TAFE. I had asked the insurance company to help with my rehabilitation to learn how to read and write again and get my brain working again. They refused to help me, demanding that I get a letter from my doctor stating that I was ready to return to work, as it would be considered training. I was so upset and frustrated with them; how could they be so mean? How could they be so small-minded? I told them, "I can't even read and write. I can hardly look after myself, let alone my two children. I am struggling with even the basics of life. How can I get a certificate to say I am ready to return to work, and how can I return if I don't get extra support and help?"

I said, "This is ridiculous; if I had a bad back, you would end up sending me to a physio. I have a bad brain; it is no different. it is just physio for my brain, and I need help."

Once again, they refused to help. I found going to TAFE and creating art great for my cognition. Not only did the art seem to help get the neurons firing again, but they also had a support system where, if you had a disability, you could get help from a tutor. Those tutors who helped me were an absolute blessing. They helped with my recovery and helped give me the skills to be a great mum; it's hard to be a parent when you can't read and write. Part of the curriculum included art history, and art history involved reading and writing. I wouldn't say I liked that subject at the time. However, reflecting on it many years later, it is funny how I now love the subject.

TAFE gave me a social outlet. My illness had caused me to lose contact with others, and I was no longer working. Having to turn up to TAFE each week got me out of the house and mixing with others. It was great, and I met some wonderful people along the way, some with whom I have remained dear friends until this day. There was one beautiful soul who I connected with, and we had so much in common. We had both been through memory loss and lost part of our lives to illness, which gave us both a determination to improve our memory and cognition as well as an incredible zest for life, fun and adventures. We also shared the same love for art and God and have been a strength and an encouragement to each other on our bad days and when we find life a struggle. Meeting each other has been such a blessing.

I also met another dear friend through art; we have strangely become friends twice. Initially, I met her through doing a short course at TAFE. Unfortunately, when we first met, it was during a time when I was having memory problems and was quite unwell. Years later, we reconnected through the Newcastle Printmakers; she recognised me at a meeting, and she seemed lovely, so I felt confident in apologising and explaining that I could not remember her and that I had memory loss. I am glad we reconnected. We live in the same suburb, and I love the walks along the beach we share and the time we spend at the Printmakers and looking at art exhibitions.

After completing my diploma, I had the same problem: finding the time to fit in creating artwork. Life was still chaotic and I was still struggling with my health, and I didn't have the discipline to find time to create. I decided to enrol in the advanced diploma program in fine arts and complete it the same way I did the diploma by doing a one-year course over three years. I loved going to TAFE, making the time to create, and learning so many new skills. I found comfort and strength in the three Ps: painting, printmaking, and photography. At the end of the course, I still needed to challenge myself a little more, so I enrolled in the Fine Art, Creative Practice Degree, which I'm still slowly working through.

Creating art has also helped with my confidence in so many ways. Over time, I have found my artwork, cognition, comprehension and communication skills improving. It has been wonderful that my artworks have become finalists and won awards in many competitions. It is also rewarding knowing that other people have enjoyed my artwork and talent and have purchased my work. I have volunteered on committees and helped at community events and workshops in the arts community, and I am now teaching others, which I love.

Art and art therapy have helped me accept and like who I am. It has allowed me to express myself and communicate with the world in ways I never thought possible, giving me confidence and strength. It has also given me the gift of patience and the ability to accept that it's OK to make mistakes (mistakes are part of art; it is how you become a better artist, and sometimes, if you are lucky, those mistakes become masterpieces). Urban sketching and en plein air painting are my favourite moments. Spending time outdoors painting or drawing gives me so much pleasure. I get to enjoy the fresh air and sunshine, and it allows me to connect with the people and the land where I am. It also gets me out of my head, away from my thoughts, which is undoubtedly a blessing some days.

My artwork, and the lack of artwork in the case of my self-portrait, gave me the ability to understand myself more and to realise that I was struggling with my identity (memory loss can do that to a person). It made me realise that I had a blockage and that I didn't like myself and the way I looked. There were a few occasions when I was tasked to do a self-portrait, drawing, painting and lino print; I could not bring myself to do it. It wasn't until later, while doing art therapy, when I had to draw myself during a happy moment as a child, that I realised what had happened. Drawing myself as a child helped me release that blockage, understand myself more, accept myself, and understand I was perfect, just like God made me. I now look forward to creating more artworks with me as the subject. Who knows, one day, I may even put it into the Archibald or Kilgore art prize.

I have discovered that art is a good way of letting go of my emotions and calming myself. Putting down random shapes, drawings and colours swirling around in my head without any rhyme or reason was therapeutic. I didn't understand why then, but after studying art therapy and seeing its benefits, I now understand. These artworks I often did in a sketchbook were not created to become masterpieces. They were made purely just for me.

Later down the track, when I had a health scare, and I was worried that I might have cancer and had to undergo major surgery, I discovered Neurographic Art. This style of art was placed in my path at the perfect time; it helped me deal with the stress and emotional tsunami occurring at the time and the difficulties I was going through in a relationship. On a positive note, the surgery went well, and it turned out that I did not have cancer. It also caused me to reassess my life and lifestyle, as I had gotten on top of things just in time before the cells had changed to cancer. I am now aware that I need to look after myself and my emotions even better to ensure this does not happen in the future.

I am so grateful that I have art in my life. The joy it has brought, the healing and growth it has created and the beautiful people that have crossed my path through TAFE, workshops and being part of art societies and the printmaker's workshop. I know it has also been a blessing to many others who have crossed my path, and I encourage anyone struggling with their health in any way to give it a go. You don't have to create a masterpiece or art for the whole world to see. My favourite art is often the artwork I have created just for myself to see.

ART AS THERAPY, THE THREE P'S

PEARLS OF WISDOM:

Creativity takes courage. (Henri Matisse)

Adding some creativity to your day is like going on a short, exciting, fun adventure, allowing you to forget your worries for a while. (Sharran Makin)

I have filled him with the spirit of God, giving him great wisdom, ability, and expertise in all kinds of craft. He is a master craftsman, expert in working with gold, silver, and bronze. He is skilled in engraving and mounting gemstones and in carving wood. He is a master at every craft. (Exodus 31:3-5)

Chapter 10

FAITH AND RELIGION

Before I lose some people here because they're not religious or the church has harmed them or someone they know in some way, please bear with me as I share my unique wisdom and a different perspective on religion. Yes, I know some people who have represented the church at times throughout history have hurt others, and they should be held accountable for their actions. People should be protected so that this does not occur again in the future. Please consider that the church has also been a blessing to many people, a place of great comfort and healing and rescuing many.

It is interesting that as I began writing this book, I was feeling confident and was looking forward to sharing some of the techniques that helped me deal with depression, anxiety, and PTSD when doctors were not able to help me. Then, suddenly, I had quite a few challenges thrown at me. I felt like I was under a spiritual attack that made me question my ability to write this book and about my faith.

I was given health challenges, needing an operation and a fair bit of bed rest, which required two weeks of not being able to drive and six weeks of not being able to lift, bend, exercise or do housework, and I needed a great deal of rest to recover. I couldn't swim or bathe, stand for long periods in the shower, exercise, or go for a massage or to the chiropractor, all things that have helped me in the past. I had to take medications that made my depression worse, and my physical injuries felt like they were worsening due to my lack of movement and need for bed rest.

I was left feeling isolated and alone, and to top it off, I was also given relationship challenges. I was in so much pain both physically and mentally and felt entirely alone once again; those who I thought would be able to help me after my operation also had challenges thrown at them that prevented them from being able to help, including one of my friends, who offered for me to stay with her and her family after my operation, having a heart attack and needing extra help herself.

FAITH AND RELIGION

It got to the point where I was feeling completely defeated. I could not do all the things that I could rely on in the past to help me due to the operation and all the restrictions that were placed on me. One day, when I felt all hope was lost, I realised there was still one thing I could do: pray and turn my focus to God. I was at home alone at the time, and I prayed. I felt a peace come over me, and I felt God telling me to go outside and sit in the sun, and I began to read the bible. As I read each page, I put beautiful, coloured pencil marks on the page, bringing together God, nature, sunlight, and art. I felt renewed; I felt the sun rays God had created penetrating my skin and healing me, along with His words.

At the time, I thought it was odd that I felt like God was telling me to go and sit in the sun. After doing this and feeling a little better, however, it allowed me to research ways to help treat jaundice naturally, which was what I was suffering from after all of the medication I was given after my operation. I was amazed that one of the primary treatments is sunshine and light therapy. God knew exactly what I needed. He told me he loves me, and that I would be ok to rest and recover and share my story in my book; that it will help many. Things started improving, and I started recovering and feeling more peace. I continued sitting in the sun, spending time with God, and praying. Over time, I slowly added the other tried and tested techniques I had used in the past. Each day, I began feeling a little better. Whilst going through all this was dreadful and challenging, I feel like this had to happen to remind me that God is certainly part of my recovery.

Like many, I struggled with the concept of religion for quite some time. I was disillusioned by it all at first. I was brought up in a non-religious home. There was a reason my mum and dad chose that for us, as the church had refused to marry them. They were in love, trying to do the right thing and get married, and the church knocked them back, as my dad was classified as bad or not good enough because he had previously been married. That was certainly not the case – he did nothing wrong and was a wonderful and good man. All he had done wrong was to make a mistake and marry the wrong person. He had dated a lady for about seven years, and their marriage lasted about seven days. She walked out on him, there were no kids, and he didn't do anything wrong. She just got cold feet and spoke out about this too late. Deciding this before the wedding certainly would have been a better option. For this, my mum and dad were judged by the church.

Eventually, they found a church that would marry them, and their marriage lasted until the day they died. So, no religion for me growing up. I certainly would not be happy if someone judged me over the fact that I was divorced, particularly since it had been taken out of my hands. My husband had an affair and chose to leave me;

FAITH AND RELIGION

if I had a choice, I would have preferred for him to let her go and work through it all and stay together as a family, but it did not turn out that way.

My mother didn't believe in God or Jesus at all. For my dad, whilst he believed in Jesus and God, religion wasn't part of his life, and I wasn't aware of his faith until towards the end of his life. It also wasn't until later in my life that I learned of Jesus, the Holy Spirit and God; oddly, though, I can remember as a child being at my grandmother's place, kneeling on the floor and praying in front of a statue and at the side of my bed. I think my mum was in hospital sick at the time. Reflecting on this, I find it strange that as a small child, praying just seemed natural, even though I was not from a religious family. Later in life, however, I had to work on it until it became natural once again.

I had a few friends earlier in my adult life who invited me to their church. It was a Catholic Church, but whilst it opened my mind to religion, something didn't seem to fit with me there, and I didn't keep going. It wasn't until I was ready to get married and I realised I hadn't been baptised that I decided to give myself to God, and I was baptised and dedicated. I was young, a shift worker, and later a mother with small children; life was hectic. I occasionally attended church, but apart from that, I didn't think much about my religion outside of church.

Eventually, I stopped attending, as the church I attended had an older congregation, and no young families attended. I had two energetic children; a toddler who was very active and couldn't sit still and loved using his vocal cords and banging things, and a baby who was also finding his voice. It felt like every time they made a noise, I had all eyes directed at me. I didn't feel like I fitted in and didn't feel welcome.

Years later, everything felt like it had fallen apart. I was a single mum, very sick and had PTSD, memory loss and chronic fatigue. I could hardly function and had lost hope as the doctors couldn't help me, and I could not find any answers – until a beautiful and kind mother of one of my son's friends asked me to attend her church. I accepted her invitation, and it felt like I had found my home; I seemed to fit in to this church. I could understand the words and the songs. There were young kids, young adults, and older adults. Everyone was welcoming, and it seemed like one big happy family. I spent more time learning about Jesus, attending bible study, and being involved in the church community.

My friends and the people at the church would have no idea that they not only helped me find God but also helped me build my self-esteem through my new friendships and social interactions (some are now like family to me), as well as the skill of being a mum. The memory loss had also taken away my knowledge and

FAITH AND RELIGION

confidence in cooking, and at the time, MasterChef was big on TV, so they would get together and have big group cook-ups, challenging each other and having fun. I was invited to attend. I cooked alongside these beautiful ladies, watching them cook and gaining new skills and confidence. I am sure my kids appreciated the new skills I had picked up: no more steak that was like eating cardboard and mushy, overcooked vegetables with no taste. Yuck!

Things seemed to be going well until, bam, my faith was challenged. When I started getting some memories back, unfortunately, all the things that had strong emotions tied to them were the things that started coming back first. You guessed it, the crappy feelings and memories from my time policing started to rear their ugly heads again. This was also at the time that there was a Royal Commission into paedophilia; this just happened to have been one of the things that tipped me over the edge towards the end of my policing career. While I had not recovered, things seemed to have been improving, and I was beginning to have hope again. Then, due to all the media reports about the Royal Commission, which highlighted the problem with paedophilia within the church, I started to lose hope and question my faith. In turn, my health started slipping back further.

How could this be? The one thing helping me was now the thing I didn't want anything to do with. There was a relentless pounding and rogue waves of emotions; it seemed that terrible things kept happening no matter what I did. It seemed like the world was ending. Everyone was so caught up in their own self, their own pain and suffering. It also seemed like no love or kindness could be found anywhere in the world.

It was interesting that just when I was stepping back from religion and the church, a commitment that I had made a year prior and had forgotten about had presented itself to me. My dear friend, who is no longer in this world and is now back home with her maker, invited me to Sydney to attend the Colour Conference, a women's religious conference. We had made this plan and booked our tickets a year earlier. I didn't have the heart to tell her that I didn't want to go with her as she had had quite the journey with battling cancer and was really looking forward to the trip. I decided to go and looked at it as an adventure and a chance to spend quality time with my friend.

Once again, I felt like I was under a spiritual attack, and something was trying to stop me from going. My friend had booked the accommodation through a booking website on the computer. It turned out that the company she had booked through had gone bankrupt, and although our accommodation had been paid for, it no longer existed. The motel would not honour the booking, telling us we would have to pay again. This

FAITH AND RELIGION

was not the only challenge we had thrown at us; we also had difficulties with public transport that day, and when I attended the conference, the security staff treated me unfairly and poorly. I needed to stand from time to time as I had a bad back. They did not like this, even though it was in an area that was not blocking anyone's view. They threatened to throw me out of the conference. Enough was enough, I thought to myself, and I asked for a refund on my tickets. I would let my friend stay and enjoy the rest of the conference, and I would go and see the sights of Sydney.

When I spoke to them about the situation, they apologised and moved my friend and me into a particular area where I could stand up and move about. I'm glad I stayed as I really felt touched and moved by the Holy Spirit during that time, and God spoke to me through prayer, giving me insightful information that could help me and others.

I felt Jesus comforting me when I felt sad and alone. He spoke to me and told me to have faith that churches are manufactured and manmade and run by humankind; humankind can be flawed and open to corruption. Have faith in God. God is not the church. While this information was passed to me, I was given images of a wolf in sheep's clothing and a Trojan horse, which was used by the Greeks during the Trojan War to trick and bring foes into a securely protected place. It felt like this was what Satan was doing to God. He could see the good happening by spreading God's word and giving hope to people, and Satan didn't like this. He planted some of his men into the church, just like the wolf in sheep's clothing and the Trojan Horse, to try and destroy God's name. God reassured me that He is not the church, and to trust in Him. I could feel his sadness. He also reassured me that not all churches had been affected.

I know some church leaders have hurt many people, and I send my love and prayers for healing to all of them. It is a shame that such leaders were able to infiltrate the churches and trick the congregation into thinking that they were a gift from God, which they indeed were not. These wolves have not only ravished their victims but also God's name, causing some people to turn away from their faith. This is a shame, as this was not God's doing but an act of evil; God has nothing but love for us. For God so loved the world, that He gave His only begotten son, that whoever believeth in Him should not perish, but have everlasting life (John 3:16).

Some places worldwide with the happiest and longest-living people have something in common: faith. In Australia, it is said that the Seven-day Adventist people are some of the happiest, healthiest, longest-living people. As a community, they have faith, a sense of community and a healthy diet. Churches can help support faith, community, and a sense of belonging. I am grateful for the Royal Commission into paedophilia and how some

FAITH AND RELIGION

church leaders have had the spotlight shined on them. Their behaviour was appalling, and it had to be stopped, and the wolves needed to be removed so that the lambs could grow to be happy and healthy.

It is up to us all to make sure these wolves and Trojan horses are not allowed back into the churches again and that people are protected. We all need to learn from the mistakes of the past, to make sure measures are in place so that the congregation, young and old, are safe and protected, to make sure that people feel safe to speak up, and to ensure that there is not just one leader but many and that there are equal numbers of both male and female leaders in a church. Parents also need to take responsibility to ensure their children are safe, involved in the church and the activities, and speak up if something does not seem right. This includes all areas of your child's life, whether it be sports, school or family and friends.

God wants the churches protected so that evil cannot penetrate its walls again and to encourage smaller congregations in more places. He is asking for more women to step up into leadership roles and have both men and women leading. He asks for strong people to stand for roles to ensure the church is protected and people stand up and speak out if something is wrong. You see, bad things happen when good people do nothing. Most of all, he would like to restore a sense of community and family to the church again and encourage people to be able to gather in smaller groups in the community or someone's home and not feel like the church is the only place where we can hear His word or feel his love for us; we can be touched by His love anywhere and anytime.

I am reminded of Jesus and how He spread God's word not just through churches but everywhere He went; people would gather outside and in people's homes to hear His word. He would speak to both individuals and groups. Whilst the church is a way to listen to God's word, it may not be for everyone. Today, there are so many more options available to hear God's word; some may feel more comfortable in a smaller setting like a bible study group in someone's home, they may feel more comfortable listening to the bible rather than reading it or even listening to a podcast or reading a book or watching a church service on TV or online. Please be aware, though, that Satan has the same resources available; be careful not to let the wrong message in.

In this time of prayer, Jesus also pointed out that there is a great deal of hurt and anger in the world and that some people are often quick to judge when they don't have all the facts and have not been given the correct information. They think that they know everything about religion and that their religion is the only religion. He reminded me that today, many countries worldwide have become very multicultural, having different cultures and different experiences throughout history.

FAITH AND RELIGION

The world is such a prominent and expansive place; its circumference is 40,075km. Long ago, travel was limited, and people stayed in their own area. Slowly, travel improved, and people travelled further abroad, often on a ship for months and months, to get to their new destination. He reminded me that long ago, people didn't venture far from their village and only had the experiences and knowledge of what happened there; there was no travel, media, or internet like nowadays. Travel has advanced so much that you can travel from one end of the world to another in a day or two. Australia and some other countries have become very multicultural, with people from many different countries and nationalities speaking many languages.

He reminded me what one country calls a chair, a different country will call something else. For example, in Greek, it is a karékla, and in French, it is called a chaise. It is also true for Him, and in some countries, they call him a different name and have had their own unique experiences throughout history. While this is beautiful, I wonder if it has caused confusion and division that need not be there. When you think about it, a German, French, Spanish, Italian, Israeli and English-speaking person would all use a different word to talk about a chair, a dog, a vehicle, etc; the same is true about God. God is meant to be everywhere and in all places, so while things would have been happening in one part of the world, God was touching people's lives in other ways in other parts of the world. As a society, we should work towards respecting this and work towards love, peace, and acceptance of each other and our differences.

With today's technology, though, we need to be careful not to be fed false information. He told me that spiritually, I would know if it was wrong or if I was being given the incorrect information as it wouldn't feel right and wouldn't come from a place of love, trust, and compassion. He also wanted us to band together, respect and care for one another, and stop worldwide wars and disputes.

I have found a beautiful church where I feel safe, protected, and supported. I know the leaders are there in God's name and for the greater good, and they want to bring good into their communities and improve people's lives. It is not about making money. Money is needed to run a building, electricity, phones, pamphlets, etc. and to have the ability to give back to the community and the less fortunate, but it is not about people needing to make a profit, so they become rich and others poor. It is about helping and supporting others and their community.

There have been many moments during my life when I really could not understand the life I was given; I was a good person, had empathy and love inside, and didn't deserve what was given to me. It seemed that after first developing PTSD, the waves kept coming, and just when I thought I was heading for the safe, quiet harbour so that

FAITH AND RELIGION

I could heal and recover, another wave would hit me; life and people kept dragging me back out to the stormy sea hoping to take me under. It has taken me until now to realise why; it appears that all the hard times I have been through have prepared me for this moment today and what the world and my country are dealing with. Many are dealing with illness for the first time, depression, anxiety, fear, job loss and financial uncertainty, and many may be grieving the loss of loved ones and having to deal with young children or teenagers while experiencing distress or having to deal with social isolation for the first time. It appears now that many people are being forced out of the safe harbour and finding themselves in those stormy seas.

For me, nothing has changed; I have had to deal with all those things already, including social isolation. Suddenly, it feels like the stormy seas have calmed, and I have made my way into the safe and calm of the harbour. I have also been reminded that while my journey was difficult (it certainly wasn't pleasant, and I didn't think it was fair), I have been moulded and shaped – just like an artist would while creating a sculpture or a pot - for this moment and other moments so that I can offer comfort to others and help them get through difficult times.

We have all been given warning signs. Our country has been through many years of drought, followed by disastrous fires, floods, deadly diseases, and more drought and floods. We have been hit with this one thing after another, and it is time we all acknowledge the warning signs. It is time we learn and grow and find love, compassion, forgiveness, and empathy. It is time we find patience and grace and be humble, give up our wicked ways to help one another, and for countries to come together and unite.

FAITH AND RELIGION

PEARLS OF WISDOM:

Don't be afraid, for I am with you. Don't be discouraged, for I am your God. I will strengthen you and help you. I will hold you up with my victorious right hand. (Isaiah 41:10)

Don't fret or worry. Instead of worrying, pray. Let petitions and praises shape your worries into prayers, letting God know your concerns. Before you know it, a sense of God's wholeness, everything coming together for good, will come and settle you down. It's wonderful what happens when Christ displaces worry at the centre of your life. (Philippians 4:6-7)

Chapter II

REFLECTING ON THE POSITIVES AND LEARNINGS

Who would have thought that after all that I had been through, I would be able to find positives from the experiences? Here are a few things I have learned that you might also find helpful or that might give you a different perspective to help you through your journey. The most important thing I have learned is that I can fly and that anything is possible with faith, tenacity, and resilience.

SHARRAN MAKIN

Learning to fly

When the explosion came in the way of PTSD and chronic pain, I tried to fight it for the sake of my two children, and I tried to beat it. It was a harrowing journey, and I could no longer fight it. It was way too strong of a force, and after years of fighting, I had no more energy and no more fight left in me. I fell hard from an enormous cliff and landed injured on a ledge that was halfway down the largest cliff face in the world, and there was no rescue party coming for me. I had three choices: I could stay there, do nothing and die, I could take that final jump and plummet to my death, or I could choose to soar like an eagle and learn to fly. I have chosen to dance with my depression and anxiety instead of fighting. I have chosen to accept it. I have chosen to learn how to fly instead of plummeting to my death. I've chosen to share my story to inspire others going through a similar journey or challenging times and give them the courage and wisdom to learn how to fly so they can also soar like eagles.

Good things can come from the bad

I've learned that good things can come from the bad. Even though it was a difficult journey for me being a single mum who was unwell and having to relearn everything when my husband left, there was a blessing that came from it. He didn't understand my memory loss. Whenever

REFLECTING ON THE POSITIVES AND LEARNINGS

I would ask him how to get somewhere or the names of the kids on my son's soccer team and other things, he would snap at me, telling me that I already knew that, rather than trying to help and support me. This only added to my anxiety, and I certainly didn't need that. He didn't try to understand my memory loss, depression, anxiety, and PTSD and that I needed to adapt things in my life to be able to cope, including avoiding different foods, drinks and alcohol as some things would make my depression and anxiety worse. You see, he could eat and drink everything, so, in his eyes, everyone else should be able to do the same.

He would encourage me to eat and drink foods that didn't agree with me. He would encourage me to take the medicines that were making me ill or worse, just because the doctors had prescribed them to me, and he couldn't think outside the square with my recovery. His leaving me has allowed me to discover new ways of healing and dealing with things, and maybe has even saved my life, as several antidepressants and painkillers certainly made me feel suicidal and like there was no way out (this is not part of my nature and was a side effect of the medications I was taking. My father had taught me there is always a solution to everything, you just have to find the right one). Reflecting on these difficult times, I have realised that I was better off having no partner than someone preventing me from getting better (maybe things may have been different if he had had this knowledge). I have learned that sometimes bad things can also become a blessing.

So now, I'm not too quick to judge something as good or bad. I'm reminded of the parable of the farmer. One day, his beautiful prize-winning mare broke loose and ran away.

"What bad luck," the neighbour said.

The farmer replied, "Maybe. Maybe not."

The next day, the mare returned with the most robust and beautiful stallion a farmer had ever seen.

"What good luck," said the neighbour.

"Maybe, or maybe not", said the farmer.

The next day, the farmer's son rode on the new stallion, who bucked him off, causing him to break his arm.

"What bad luck," said the neighbour.

"Maybe. Maybe not," said the farmer.

The next day, the government came around, recruiting all the young men in the community to go off and fight in the war. The father's son, having a broken arm, was not taken.

REFLECTING ON THE POSITIVES AND LEARNINGS

"What good luck," said the neighbour.

In this story, there is a variety of good and bad that occurs, from something that is looked at as bad in the beginning and even towards the end with the farmer's son having a broken arm, which is undoubtedly painful and restrictive in many ways and what many would see as something bad. But the broken arm turned out a blessing as the farmer's son was saved from going to war. It possibly saved his life, and he could still help his dad on the farm when he recovered from his break. Really, who am I to judge what is good or bad?

I remember an incident where several obstacles out of my control got in my way, causing me to be late to visit a dear friend I grew up with and had not seen for maybe 20 years or more. His wife had recently died. I didn't want to be late, and I remember getting angry and frustrated at the time. Then, whilst I was driving to see him, I drove past a fatal car accident. I remember becoming very thankful for the things that had held me back that day, causing me to run late. I may have been in that accident if I had been on time.

I have had another two incidences since when I was running late. I remember calling into a shop one day in Murrurundi when I returned home from one of my big adventures; I always loved looking around the shops and galleries there. I remember crossing paths with a beautiful, kind woman who needed extra support that day when I stopped at one of the shops. She was going through a tough time and thought I was a caring ear who would listen to her. I listened to her story compassionately. I remember thinking partway through that I needed to get on the road. It was starting to get dark, and I didn't want to drive at night in the country where kangaroos, pigs, and deer could run out in front of me and cause an accident. I was frustrated that I hadn't gotten on the road, but I was also grateful that I could listen and help somebody in need. I drove about 20 minutes down the road and came across a horrific accident. The carnage was terrible; I am not sure if there was a fatality, but there were people badly injured. Once again, I am very grateful that I was delayed that day. As I said, who am I to judge what is good or bad?

Empathy and compassion

I've learned empathy, compassion, and understanding. I believe I was a good police officer and probably gave people more chances than others would. I did feel for people and have empathy. However, I didn't understand how someone would turn to drugs and alcohol or could be a perpetrator or a victim of domestic violence and stay in a bad relationship. Why did people commit crimes?

You see, life had been relatively sweet for me growing up. I may not have come from a rich and famous family,

REFLECTING ON THE POSITIVES AND LEARNINGS

but I came from a family where my mum, dad and grandparents had stuck by each other in richness and poorness and during sickness and health. And I didn't witness any domestic violence. I was always provided for, and food was always on the table. I have always lived in humble homes, but in such beautiful places where there was plenty of nature and fresh air, with opportunities for lots of fun, adventures and exploring. Besides moving around too much and having to keep making new friends, life was sweet.

As a result of my experiences of being a police officer, along with the journey that I was given with my health, PTSD, depression, anxiety and memory loss, I now have a different perspective on life and people. I now understand how and why people can become the way they are. I also know that with the proper knowledge and support, and if they have people who believe in them, people can change for the better for themselves and their families.

I am now more humble and able to accept my flaws and those of others. I have learned that forgiving and letting go is better than holding on. That doesn't mean I won't protect myself and others or avoid being placed in a bad situation again, and it doesn't mean I won't stand up for myself, my family, or others. I certainly will, but holding on to the crap that has already happened that you cannot change or fix weighs you down, and it becomes smelly.

SHARRAN MAKIN

Importance of communication

I've learnt the importance of communication. Talking about a situation and problem is much better than shutting the other person out, and if something is eating me up inside, not communicating can sometimes worsen the problem. Two people can be correct, and two people can be wrong. One person can be right and the other wrong. At least if you take the time to talk, you can understand why something has happened, the other person can understand why they were wrong, or a solution to a problem can be found.

One day, I was reminded of this while driving with my brother in the car. I was the driver, and I was turning into a shopping centre car park. My brother had a dig at me, telling me I had just broken the law and couldn't turn into the car park like that. I told him he was wrong and that I could. He said that he is a professional driver and knows the rules better than I do. This could have turned into an argument, and I did not want to argue with him. I thought he was wrong, and he thought I was wrong. It was good that I had a curious mind and a desire to learn, and I also didn't want to break the law in any way, so I looked up the answer. I laughed when I did, as it turned out that we were both right. You see, I lived in New South Wales, and he lived in Queensland, two different states with two different rules.

REFLECTING ON THE POSITIVES AND LEARNINGS

I wonder how many friendships and families could have been saved through communication. I wonder how many wars could have been prevented if people had just taken the time to communicate and understand each other. I also wonder how many domestic and neighbour disputes I attended as a police officer could have been avoided if people had learned to be more empathetic, have loving, compassionate hearts, be curious, and communicate better to understand each other.

Many fights between families, friends, businesses, and countries could have been solved or avoided altogether with respect and communication. Sometimes, living in Australia can be a little challenging regarding communication. I love how multicultural we are; each culture brings something unique and special. However, it can also have challenges, as sometimes it has caused misunderstandings between families, friends, and communities. I didn't understand this until recently when I met someone who had migrated to Australia as a child and had a different nationality than me. He complained that I didn't understand him or his culture and that he had suffered this challenge with people all his life.

It made me reflect on a dear friend and neighbour who meant so much to me, and who I now miss having in my life. She was also an immigrant from another country. One day, she took offence to how I greeted her on the phone. I could not understand it; she was like family to me, so I thought I could speak to her the same way I would talk to my family. At the time, my family would say, "Hello, how are you? What's the goss?" At the time, she thought I was accusing her of being a gossiper. I certainly wasn't. I loved her so much, it was just a playful way that my family and I communicated at the time. Sadly, she is no longer in my life. However, I have stood up for her with others when she needed extra support and expressed to them how she has done many great things for her community.

I have since made a beautiful new friendship with a lady from the same culture. We have much in common with our art, being women of faith and sharing the same challenge with memory loss. Because of this, we know that we would never say the wrong thing or try to hurt each other or someone else, and we can ask questions if needed to understand and support each other more. At the beginning of our friendship, we had both sometimes gotten the meaning of some words wrong or sometimes had words that had different meanings from our own cultures. We both have a curious mind and a thirst for learning (that comes from the experience of memory loss, I think), and we both have kind hearts that want to support each other. We have learned so much from each other because of this.

I don't always get it right, as sometimes it is hard. However, I now try so much harder to understand

REFLECTING ON THE POSITIVES AND LEARNINGS

another person and try to communicate better. I have learned that not everyone is the same, that some people have not yet learned compassion and empathy and don't want to try and understand each other, and that sometimes I need to step back and not argue a point they won't understand. Rather than being angry at that person, I feel compassion for them and hope they will someday understand and have empathy, a kind heart, and a curious mind.

I will also never believe a rumour, as the person telling it often won't have all the facts or is doing it with an agenda. I've had people ask me to stay away from others, or tell me that they won't attend a function or hang out with me if I remained friends with someone because they didn't like that person. It is odd how often the person I am told to avoid is more caring and loyal than the person who told me to avoid them. Don't get me wrong, I have also been given the correct information sometimes. However, I would be cautious and curious and decide for myself. I am glad I have chosen to do things this way. I have had some beautiful souls come into my life and my kids' lives who wouldn't have been there if I had just listened to rumours and hadn't taken the time to communicate.

SHARRAN MAKIN

Thinking outside the box and having a curious mind

I've learned to think outside the box. The mainstream medicine and food most of our modern population eats or takes don't work for me. It is probably not even working for them, and they have just not realised it yet; many people are suffering from ailments, cancers, and other health problems. Unfortunately, they accept them and don't question how they can do things better and improve their quality of life.

If I hadn't gotten curious and thought outside the square regarding my recovery, maybe, just maybe, I would not be alive today. Sometimes, it can be good to walk a path already taken, as it can cut out a great deal of time and having to learn things. Sometimes, however, if the path is not working and it is causing you pain and suffering, maybe we need to make our own path, or perhaps we can find a way to improve on something, or do things a better way. It is okay to choose a different path, and yes, it may be hard work, but sometimes, the rewards, the experiences, and the views are well worth it.

Love and compassion

I've learnt to love and accept myself and, in turn, others. I have hated being alone, and I encourage you not to

REFLECTING ON THE POSITIVES AND LEARNINGS

push loved ones away so they have the same experience as I did, as it can also go the other way. Being alone and isolated can cause some people to want to give up on life and to quit, and possibly even to take their life. I often wonder how many suicides that I had to attend as a police officer could have been prevented if someone had shown that person a little love, support, and compassion. Through experience and research, I have learned that love and connection are essential for all people.

As a society, we really do need to think about how we treat people. There have been a lot of good lives lost throughout the world by suicides, mass killings and shootings caused by people criticising, bullying, alienating, and leaving people out. I also wonder how many wars could have been prevented by communication, kindness, and empathy. While I felt like giving up at first, what was the point of being here alone? I then realised it was a blessing. I was feeling weakened from all I had been through.

I was more vulnerable, having my family constantly criticising me and telling me to go and get a job, find a man, oh, you should have done this, or you should have done that. You shouldn't have done that, don't do that, don't talk about this, don't talk about that, don't tell me, you can't, don't eat that, don't go away on holiday, it won't be safe, don't learn about that, they will brainwash you, don't buy a van, don't go on that holiday, the list goes on. I didn't realise it was making my already fractured self-esteem worse. And I was feeling like a failure. What they didn't realise was that all the things that they were telling me not to do were the things that helped me with my recovery, including God.

I had tried to work or volunteer several times but couldn't. Believe me, I wanted to work, but my body and mind needed love, nurturing and time to heal. They had no idea. They had never had memory loss or damage to their brain, PTSD or depression and anxiety, divorce, nor had they been a single mum whilst unwell.

My family would say to me, "Oh, there are people worse off than you in this world; such and such's daughter is fighting cancer at the moment". I do understand that there are a great deal of people suffering from all kinds of health conditions, and I certainly do know the journey with cancer is a hard one. However, what a lot of people don't realise is that so is someone's journey with depression. I know of families that will not even acknowledge this, but depression can kill, just like cancer does; all you need to do is go onto the internet and look at the statistics.

The Lifeline website states that in 2022, about 9 Australians will die every day from suicide, which is more than double the road toll. Quite often, someone going through depression or anxiety needs someone to listen to them and encourage them with love and support. They don't

REFLECTING ON THE POSITIVES AND LEARNINGS

want someone to solve the problem or scold them and tell them that what they are going through isn't significant and that there are people worse off than them, which will probably make them feel worse, not better. You will be surprised how beneficial a simple hug or a smile can be to someone struggling.

Being on my own, away from all the noise, made me realise that whilst I had been unwell and had a lot of crappy things happen and I had not been able to return to the woman I once was, that the woman I am today is extraordinary. I have a lot to offer the world, just in a different way. I am full of love and empathy, and I care about people and the world they live in. I have touched many people's lives, improving their lives and circumstances. And while I may have had some downtime, I will continue to do so now and into the future. I realised that to do this, I needed to love and accept myself and open my heart again to a world so cold and cruel, causing me to put up a protective wall. If I let down my wall, maybe others will follow, and the world will no longer feel so cold and cruel.

I don't think my family realised what they were doing. I don't think they were doing it intentionally. I believe that it was just that they didn't know how to deal with it, and maybe deep down, they were a little scared as my healing was taking way longer than they expected. At least I'm aware of it now and will not allow it to happen again. When the time was right, I started to let people back into my life, made new friends, and formed stronger bonds with old ones.

During my isolation, I also realised the importance of love and connection and the need to support and build each other up, which I now try to do with anyone who crosses my path. I urge you to all think about the way you communicate with others. We are all trying to do our best with what we are given; shutting people out or telling someone to get a job or a man or that there are people worse off than them in the world will not fix someone or get them better. Loving and kind words and supportive actions will.

The importance of creativity and nature for healing

I have learned the importance of creativity and nature in healing. I was blessed to have the opportunity to travel several times over the last few years. On each occasion, I was surrounded by nature and a group of beautiful, fun, loving, supportive people, and I knew at once I needed more of this in my life. I have learned that connecting with nature and creativity is crucial to my recovery. Creating is healing, as is spending time in nature and sunshine. I have learnt that it takes all the noise and chaos away.

REFLECTING ON THE POSITIVES AND LEARNINGS

I'm sure many people have already found this out. For some people who suffer from depression and anxiety or have brain damage, everything is amplified: noise, smell, touch, taste, and sight. For me, sometimes being in a cafe or restaurant with all the noise and chatter and the baristas making coffee can make me feel like I'm in the middle of a war zone with bombs and guns going off in every direction. A TV or music that is too loud can feel like an explosion echoing through your head and body. Kids fighting and arguing can feel like being stuck in a tunnel with a freight train going through it, a train that you know will strike you down at the end. Wearing clothes too tight could send me into anxiety and panic. My point is that everything is amplified, and somehow, being in nature, in fresh air, near the ocean or submerged in water at the beach, a lake, river, or dam seems to ground me. It seems to make things better. I learned this early in my recovery, which I am grateful for now. It has been my saviour and has influenced my decision on where to live.

I've also discovered the healing power of art and creativity. It is nice to create art just for the sake of creating art. I found it a great way of dealing with stress and getting my brain working again. It is weird; sometimes, depression can take over, and I cannot find any inspiration to create or paint. However, I have sometimes found myself in the deepest, darkest places and felt like I couldn't get out. I discovered that drawing and painting random stuff, shapes, and colours in my head was a way to bring me back out of the turmoil.

Learning the power of humour

I discovered the importance of having a sense of humour and being able to laugh at yourself. Unfortunately, I'd become quite serious due to my circumstances. There was a lot that I had to wade through; man, it was like a jungle out there. I had to learn to protect myself and my kids as I was in fear that all my cubs could be eaten. I felt very self-conscious about my memory and often tried to hide this from people who crossed my path. While walking, I would have people come up to me and chat. They knew who I was and who my kids were, but I had no idea who they were. It was scary for me. I would keep the conversation simple, answer their questions, ask them how they were and excuse myself, saying I had to keep moving.

There came a moment when I finally found myself able to lighten up over the whole thing. It was when a lady came up to me in the shopping centre. She knew so much about me, where I lived, and my kids; I had no idea who she was, so I kept the conversation simple again. This time, I had my son out shopping with me, and I was curious about this lady who knew so much about me. She would have had to have been close to me. By that stage, I was starting to remember anyone who had touched my heart and with whom I had a solid connection.

So why couldn't I remember this one? I asked my son who the lady was. He told me it was the father of a young girl my sons had been friends with and who used to live across the road from us. "Mum, he had a sex change." I have no disrespect for transgender communities, and I have respect for all sexualities, but I laughed and laughed and laughed at myself all the way home. I had been so hard on myself for not remembering who this lady was, but of course, I wouldn't have recognised her, as she was a he when I had placed her. How could I have known? Plus, he looked so feminine and beautiful at the time I didn't realise I was speaking to a man. It was from this moment I started to lighten up on myself.

I now love it when somebody tells me a good joke, and I love reading the jokes a dear friend of mine posts on Facebook each day. I also try to put a little humour into my day. Not everyone gets my jokes and wit, but that's okay. I often draw a little cartoon of a scenario in my imagination to put a different perspective on life or situations.

I have learned I have a voice

I've learned to stand up for myself and others. After the pain and suffering I have seen myself and others go through, I have learned that I do have a voice. I really cannot just sit back and watch anymore. I've learned that bad things happen to good people when good people do nothing. If I do something that doesn't work, at least I've tried, and that's important.

I have learned not to rely on others for the answers to get me well and that the government, police, doctors, lawyers, etc. are not always correct nor do they have all the answers, and do not always keep their promises. Many lawyers have torn families apart and encouraged them to fight and not speak when speaking was just what was needed and would have seen a better outcome for all of them. The family would have remained intact, and everyone would have been okay, realising there was no reason to fight. Some people have gotten sick from the stress of fighting legal battles that could have easily been solved through negotiation and communication.

I have seen police leave children at risk of harm. I have also seen police take away a disabled child from their parents, who are loving and kind and good parents – this happened just because they were thinking outside the box to try and get their child well and not have him die like doctors told them would happen in a few years. Could they really have been that bad as parents given that the government left the other two children with the parents, and they are happy and healthy? If they were that bad as parents, why didn't the police take the other

REFLECTING ON THE POSITIVES AND LEARNINGS

two children? This child, not a baby, was deficient in a vitamin. The parents refused to give him formula for the rest of his life and chose to blend meals and give him fresh, healthy, preservative, and additive-free food. Wow, I so get this, given my journey and inability to eat processed foods and vitamins.

I was so grateful it was not me having to attend that job and take the child from his parents. The disabled child wasn't meant to live long, and the parents were trying to save their son and give him a longer and better life. Wouldn't a better option be to teach the parents the correct food they needed to provide the child with to increase the vitamin he was deficient in rather than taking the child from the parents and sisters and them not seeing him until years later after the matter went through court? This child was being cared for by strangers in a motel for years, with no family contact. Children can be such fussy eaters; I am sure millions of children out there are deficient in a vitamin or two.

I have seen the government make mistakes and break promises during my life. A representative for the police force spoke to the media years ago, stating that 'The Forgotten 300 Police', who were disadvantaged because the police force changed insurance companies between when they were injured on duty and when they were discharged, would be looked after and compensated. Many years down the track, these police have never been compensated, and 'The Forgotten 300' are still forgotten today.

Going through the coronavirus pandemic has also raised my eyebrows over some of our government's decisions. I won't go into them all, as I am sure we all have our own views on this. It was disappointing, though, witnessing people who had been on long-term unemployment getting paid more than someone who was hurt on duty as a police officer protecting and serving our community. I think the government should be ashamed of themselves.

I have also learned that doctors don't always have the answers, and sometimes, we need to speak up and take our health into our own hands. I have seen this not only with my health but also with my parents and son. My dad was diagnosed with lung cancer and given three months to live. Dad kept telling the doctors that they had it wrong, that he'd had cancer previously, and he didn't think it was cancer. No one would listen to him. He was given morphine to ease his pain, but when they did this, it looked like he would be lucky to last three weeks, let alone three months. He stopped taking the morphine and replaced it with medicinal cannabis (which he had to get on the black market as even though it had just been made legal in Australia, he couldn't get a doctor that was able to prescribe it). He finally started to look better, still suffering but doing better than what he was before.

REFLECTING ON THE POSITIVES AND LEARNINGS

Years went by, and he still complained to the doctors that they were missing something; no one would listen as they didn't expect him to live as long as he did. My dad, with a curious mind, even though he would never get the answer, decided to organise and pay for his autopsy when he died, something which would not have generally happened due to his diagnosis. Sadly, he never got the results; the results came back that he didn't have one bit of cancer in his body and that he died of pneumonia. It was so sad, and my mum passed away three months later. She had lost her will to live with not having her husband in her life.

I had a similar experience with my eldest son. I saw him suffering, in pain and struggling to be able to walk. He had to slide along the ground on his bum down the driveway as he could not walk due to pain and restrictions from hurting his knee. Now, let me tell you that that is very unusual behaviour from my kids, as they are tough, they don't get knocked down from something minor. They are the type of kids that would still be running along with blood gushing from them and not stopping or thinking anything of it until weeks later when it had become infected. I told him to go to the doctor; he replied that he had just come from the doctor and that the doctor told him everything was okay and did nothing for him. After telling him that doctors can sometimes get things wrong, my gut feeling was that the doctor had missed something and that he should trust his gut and go to the hospital if he thought something was wrong. He went to the hospital and returned with crutches and his leg in a splint. Two days later, his knee was operated on. That first doctor had made a big misdiagnosis.

I am not saying that all doctors, police, solicitors, etc. are bad, as many great ones do a fantastic job, and our world is undoubtedly a much better place because of them. I'm just saying that some may not care or have the knowledge or experience, and they may not always have all the answers. Sometimes, they get things wrong, and if something doesn't seem right, speak up or change and go to someone who can help. Make your own path if you feel like all the paths are blocked. You really matter, and sometimes, it's a path you make for yourself that can make all the difference. I paid for my own rehabilitation, I did my own art therapy, and I researched the things that could help me to get better and paid for them myself as I couldn't get the help I needed, and I needed to be well so I could be the best mum I could be. In the end, I spoke up when the medicines were making me worse or causing me to feel suicidal and said, "NO". I was worth it, and so were my children.

Mistakes are ok

I have learned that it's OK to make mistakes, and f*** up; it is how we learn and grow. Being a perfectionist and fearing failure will undoubtedly hold me back; I know I tend to do both. If we all gave up after our first fall when trying to walk as babies, we would never be walking and doing what we do today. We would have had many falls, and some have probably hurt us, but we kept going and didn't care what anyone thought. This hit me as an adult; here I was, having to learn to read and write again when all the other adults could already do this, including my kids. It was hard. I often avoided it where I could, fearing being judged or criticised. Then, one day, I just had to say f*** it; if I didn't give it a go, I would be stuck where I was forever. I learned and grew from my mistakes, and there were quite a few, believe me.

I also learned to ask for help and pay for extra help when needed and not be embarrassed or afraid to do so. I find the same thing with being an artist. Sometimes, you need to make that initial mark or put down that first brush stroke, and if it doesn't work out, that is OK. If it is not a masterpiece, so be it. I don't have to show it to anyone, at least I gave it a go, and occasionally I do get that masterpiece. I believe many people have been held back from greatness due to perfectionism or fear of failure; it is not just me who has to deal with that.

Part mermaid or fish?

I have learned I could possibly be part mermaid or fish. Sometimes, I need to make time to get my gills wet and swim in salt water. I have discovered that saltwater can wash away any troubles or worries. Before I injured my back and became unwell and pre-kids, I was a scuba diver. I did a lot of dives in beautiful places locally and around the world and even made it to the qualification of the dive master. I felt at home under the sea and at peace, but unfortunately, due to my memory loss, I had forgotten this part of my life until some years ago, when I was invited to go on a holiday with a group of beautiful and amazing women to Hawaii. They also loved the ocean and encouraged me to build up my fitness and do a bit of snorkelling before our holiday.

Wow. The first time I put my snorkel and fins on to practice was in the lake at Belmont Baths. There wasn't much to see that day, I saw water, seaweed, and the occasional boring-looking fish. For me, however, it was like diving on a tropical island with the most exciting colourful fish and coral; memories started flooding back from the time I spent under the sea when I was younger. I was finally in a place where I felt like I belonged. I now make some time to spend in the water, even in winter. During one of the nicer days in winter, you will see me having a splash in the lake or the ocean. I can now pick up on the signs that it is time to get those gills wet and wash away all those troubles.

REFLECTING ON THE POSITIVES AND LEARNINGS

PEARLS OF WISDOM:

If you have knowledge, let others light their candles in it. (Margaret Fuller)

Laughter is timeless, imagination has no age, and dreams are forever. (Walt Disney)

Be kind to each other, tender-hearted, forgiving one another, just as God through Christ has forgiven you. (Ephesians 4:32)

Chapter 12

MAKING THIS WORLD A BETTER PLACE

I am not perfect, but as I have stated in previous chapters, I am perfectly imperfect. I have made mistakes in the past, but one thing I strive to achieve is remembering that I am a WIP – a Work in Progress. I am that artwork that still needs to be finished. Each day, I try to become a better me and make small changes to improve who I am, hoping to become that masterpiece someday. Yes, some days I may get frustrated that things haven't turned out how they should have, that I have not gotten the support I needed, or that life has been unfair to me or my kids. When I get a chance to calm down and reflect, I remind myself that I am not the only work in progress in the world, and I remember that we are all trying to do the best we can with the knowledge we have at the time. I try to learn from this and sometimes pass on some of my wisdom to others (I must remember that only some are ready to learn, and sometimes I must practice patience). I encourage you all to strive to be that WIP, to make those constant small changes, moulding yourself into that beautiful masterpiece we are all capable of becoming.

When someone is frustrating you, try and show a little empathy and compassion. We don't know what people are going through at the time. I'm sure I was misunderstood on many occasions in the past. People thought because I looked normal, that I was the same strong and confident person I was in the past; they didn't try to understand how hard it was to get through being a single mum with PTSD, depression, chronic fatigue, allergies and memory loss. I wish people had shown me a little more empathy.

I was reminded of this recently when I was confronted with a woman who was angry, bossy, and rude towards me. I didn't react at the time, but in the back of my head, I thought, what a *****. It was interesting a few months later; she was surprisingly placed in my path again at a workshop I attended. When I initially worked out who she was, I thought to myself, I want to avoid this woman today. She came up to me and attempted to make conversation, and my response was to be short but polite in my answer so that she didn't hang around. After a while, I overheard a conversation she was having with another lady; tears welled in my eyes when I realised that in the initial discussion I had with her months prior, she was struggling with her emotions as her partner had just died. I finally realised the reason for her rudeness and her behaviour. She had no idea who I was or that she had been rude and nasty towards me. I later went up, conversed with her, and encouraged her with her artwork. Sometimes, we have no idea how hard life can be for others, and we shouldn't be too quick to judge or react harshly. I wish others could have shown the same compassion during my darkest times.

I often wonder how different history could be if family, friends, and society had treated some of our past world leaders and offenders differently when they were younger or at various stages throughout their lives. I wonder if communication and a bit of empathy, love, compassion, and support from family, friends, teachers, mentors or even strangers could have prevented some of the mass murders, world wars or terrorist acts that have occurred in the past or even our future. Many people behind such events have had quite a challenging past and did not receive the love and support they needed.

This is not an excuse for those challenged or mistreated to hurt others or create havoc. Use it as a wake-up call and do things differently, try and make this world a better place. There was one stage in my life where many people hurt me, and I was not given the love and support I needed. All I could see was bad in this world; my job as a police officer had also taken its toll on me. I constantly saw people at their worst and attended incidents where a tragedy or something terrible had occurred. There was a war going on, people being bashed, thieving, drugs, families being torn apart, no one having respect or kindness towards each other, and kids being abused. I remember thinking I could not handle this anymore, and I didn't want to live in a world like this any longer. I can remember weighing up the options. If I wasn't here anymore or became a hermit, my kids and even my future grandchildren would still be left in this world with all the same problems. How could I leave them alone in this kind of world without trying to improve it for them?

I have also seen how devastating it is for families and friends who have lost loved ones to suicide and the toll it takes on the emergency service workers attending these kinds of jobs. It is challenging work, I have seen way too much of this in the past, and there was no way in the world I was going to do this to anyone, especially not my kids. There was also the option of becoming cold-hearted and callous like others; however, that wasn't a solution either. If I did that, it would just add to the world's problems. I could have left things the way they were, but that wouldn't work either, as I was miserable, and I was certainly not going to remain that way. Instead, I chose to keep going. I had my challenges to deal with, so I felt

MAKING THIS WORLD A BETTER PLACE

at the time I couldn't do anything huge to change the world, but what I could do was choose to forgive those who had wronged and hurt me. I decided to do small acts of kindness along the way, giving compliments or a smile to loved ones and strangers, complimenting staff for their excellent service, checking in on friends or loved ones, or helping someone in need.

Through my experience of being a police officer and working with young offenders and children at risk, and through my challenges with memory loss, depression, and PTSD, I have had the opportunity to see the world differently. I can see many cracks, and I fear that if changes are not made soon, there may no longer be a world for my children, grandchildren, or great-grandchildren. I may not have all the answers and solutions, but I know if I encourage you to ask the question: what would the world look like if we ....? (You fill in the blanks.) My generation may not have all the answers; my kids or even their kid's generation may come up with the solutions. I hope as a community and by working together, we find the solutions to keep humanity going into the future.

I encourage more sceptics in the world and less cynics; I encourage you to ask yourselves, is what we are currently doing working, and if not, how can we do it better? Remember, if it were not for the sceptics in the world, we would probably not have automobiles, electricity, phones, and so many other things we have today. Just because a leader, mentor, or parent in the past did something a certain way, it does not necessarily mean that they had it right or had all the answers. Some may have had many of the answers, so we need to learn from what they got right and find ways to improve on things they got wrong.

I was reminded of this some time ago when I was listening to a group discussion with some young single mothers. I had some background information on these mothers before the conversation occurred. One of them was confiding in another on ways to deal with her daughter's behaviour, which was challenging at the time. The other mother replied, "Oh, it's easy, you just need to do what your parents did". Knowing the background of this young single mother who was giving advice and that she had not long beforehand had her children removed from her custody due to child protection issues, I gently intervened. I suggested to both parents that their parents did the best they could at the time with the knowledge and wisdom that they had. However, I also suggested that sometimes our parents don't always get things right, and some may have done things that were not in their children's best interest or safety. Today, we have more information and support groups available to parents than our parents had. We can reflect on what our parents may have done well and admire and build on that, and we can also look at areas where our parents didn't quite get things right and improve on that. This allows us to be the best mums or dads we can be with the knowledge

MAKING THIS WORLD A BETTER PLACE

we have. I saw a light bulb go on in their heads, and a smile came over their faces as they agreed and thanked me for my wisdom.

I have seen a broken system in many areas: health, education, law, justice, and society. I've seen too many broken families, families torn apart due to grief, greed, and miscommunication, or simply because somebody was bored and thought that the grass would be greener elsewhere.

I know that the family dynamics can sometimes change through no fault of our own, and sometimes things are taken out of our hands. Sometimes, a loved one dies way too soon, or a partner may have to end a marriage as their partner is physically or mentally abusive. No person should stay in an abusive relationship, but today, too many marriages end due to a lack of communication and them not wanting to put in the hard work to reap the rewards later. They may blame boredom or be attracted to the next shiny thing.

As a community, we need to ask, what if we supported each other through the tough times and encouraged communication and the mending of relationships? Could this help our society as a whole and have it functioning better, being happier and healthier and raising more optimistic and healthier children, encouraging them to make healthier life choices rather than turning to destructive risk-taking behaviour or taking drugs (which, instead of making life better, destroys it)?

I have heard so many adults say that if they divorce, it is ok; it doesn't affect the kids. They are only kids, and they will be okay; they bounce back. Well, maybe as a society, we need to ask, is this really the case? Yes, some do get through unscathed and achieve great things, but many don't. We must ask ourselves, could this behaviour be harming our kids? Could this be part of the problem in our society today with increased youth crime, the increase of drug and alcohol abuse or even the increase of children and adults suffering from depression and anxiety? During my time as a police youth liaison officer, I saw many kids struggling to cope in broken families. When I was on my journey of healing my PTSD, I would attend some self-help seminars and group counselling sessions. It was sad to see so many people, now adults, seeking help to deal with depression and anxiety, many blaming their childhood and their parents divorcing.

I know that there are many families already affected by divorce, and so many had no choice in the matter as it was thrown upon them. If this is the case, ask yourselves, what can I do now to support my children the best I can and help bring them up as well-functioning members of our society, being happy and healthy? This may include having quality time with your kids and making sure they can spend time with both sides of the family. They may spend extra time with grandparents, aunts, or uncles to learn the importance of family. It may be negotiating and agreeing with each parent on the foods you feed your kids, a study schedule or agreeing on ways to discipline your kids and best support each other. Yes, it is essential to share memorable and fun moments with your kids, but remember that you are still the parent, and it is good to have boundaries and discipline when needed.

It's also important to ask yourselves, how can I improve things for the next generation coming through? It could be dealing with your baggage through counselling and self-development, encouraging communication and learning, teaching your kids ways to communicate and problem solve, and teaching them the importance of family. Remember, the places in the world that have the happiest and healthiest people all have family and a sense of community and belonging in common.

Our future sceptics may find a solution to the medical problems we are having today. They may ask if we're helping or creating more problems by what is being done. Could we solve these health problems differently through education, diet, support, and hard work rather than prescribing a medication that may cause more problems? It may be that we look at what materials we are using in our everyday lives, where we are living or the materials that our home or workplace is made from. Maybe it is the clothes we wear and the chemicals that are used in the process, maybe it is what our furniture is coated with (many have been linked to cancer and other health problems).

Possibly, the up-and-coming sceptics may discover that God did have it right in the first place when he made the world and the food we eat and that humankind is contributing to many of our health problems today, including cancer, autoimmune diseases, depression and anxiety with genetically modified and chemical-laden foods. (I can remember eating ice-cream one day and reacting badly to it. I looked up the ingredients and found that one of the colours in the food was linked to cancer, depression, and headbanging in kids. The rest of the container went straight in the bin, there was no way I was going to let my kids eat that.) Or they may discover that, as a society, we are spending too much time on the computer, iPad and phones and watching too much television and find that we need to get back to nature, walking barefoot and having more simplicity in our lives.

The up-and-coming sceptics may find that we need to shake up the education system to offer more support to students and teachers, find new ways of discipline, bring the community and families together and create a sense of belonging. They may encourage different teaching and learning styles to accommodate all student's learning styles and ensure that no child is left behind and that every child is included academically and socially.

MAKING THIS WORLD A BETTER PLACE

I have seen children flourish and thrive and develop a new passion for learning under the guidance of a good and encouraging teacher and school principal, some getting the best teacher they have ever had as late as Year 11 and 12, changing the course of their lives. I have also seen wonderful kids who ended up with grumpy teachers who only had a year left until retirement and really didn't want to be there. These teachers did not give the kids the support, kindness and nurturing they needed during difficult times, instead choosing to yell at them, throw things at them, kick them out of the classroom and even suspend them from school, causing them to lose interest in school and authorities. Schools and teachers have such huge impacts on our kids lives and shaping our communities.

Future sceptics may find new ways of removing the red tape that is holding us back as a society and in the workforce, see better ways to support emergency service workers by ensuring they are more than just a number or find new ways to address social and society's needs. They may find new solutions to be able to reduce crime and help those who are struggling with drug addiction and cannot get help as there are not enough facilities available to be able to help them and their families. All in all, they may find a way to make life better for all.

I have seen many families struggling, unable to find help for their kids who have either a drug addiction or mental health challenges. Some have even become violent, and parents are still unable to get help they need as there is not enough support available. These kids and families would be much better being supported in the earlier stages, helping them, and giving them the skills they need to grow and thrive, rather than leaving it until it is too late when they have already broken the law or injured someone. Maybe the up-and-coming sceptic may have a vision to bring other professions – for example doctors, counselling, and social workers – into the education district, working together to help these children thrive.

I encourage you all to get creative with your thinking and problem-solving. We may find a new and better solution to all sorts of things and have a future where no woman, man or child is left behind, and we all get along and live in peace and harmony. A world where there is no shortage of food, water, and shelter, and everyone feels essential and belongs, which may lead to a future with less crime, drugs, war, and terrorism. Who knows what is possible?

MAKING THIS WORLD A BETTER PLACE

PEARLS OF WISDOM:

*If you can dream it, you can make it happen!
(Unknown)*

Each day, make small changes to improve who you are, and become that masterpiece you are all capable of being. (Sharran Makin)

Look at each day as a new blank canvas; you can paint it any way you choose. (Sharran Makin)

AFTERWORD

Everyone's life journey is different. Try not to compare yourselves to others, and if you are going to compare, compare yourself to yourself, making those constant small changes each day. You will be surprised how quickly those small changes add up. Yes, there may be some bad days or setbacks, but that is okay; you take the time you need, be patient, and do what you need to get yourself back on track.

If you or a loved one is struggling, know that you are not alone and that many others are also struggling. You may not notice them as they probably are wearing that mask of false bravado or hiding away from the world on their bad days. Know that it is okay to ask for help if you need it. Suffering from depression or anxiety is no different to having an injury or illness to any other part of your body that someone may ask for help for, and as a society, we need to remove the stigma attached to it.

If anything comes up in this book that you can relate to and wonder if you could have done things differently, don't feel bad that you didn't; instead, use it as a time to reflect and learn and work out solutions to how you can do things differently now and into the future. Remember, we are all a work in progress, and you are never too old to stop learning and growing.

If you are struggling, please reach out to someone you trust, your doctor if needed or a new doctor if you have lost confidence in your old doctor. Find a good counsellor or life coach or reach out to one of the helplines like Lifeline, Kids Helpline or the Black Dog Institute.

Most importantly, I encourage you to be kind and love yourself and others. Have empathy, compassion, strength, and wisdom. Forgive yourself and others and move forward to live the best life possible, being the best version of yourself that you can be. Keep the faith and believe that there are better days ahead.

While I have had quite the journey and many darker days, I am so grateful to be alive today. My journey is not over, and although I have travelled so far, I still have quite the way to go. I still must watch what I eat, keep my stress levels in check and follow the tips that I have

AFTERWORD

written about. Yes, it is hard work and I miss out on many yummy foods that others get to enjoy, and I have had to make many sacrifices. It has been worth it though, and life is much better than it has been in the past. When those challenging days sneak in, I remind myself to celebrate the good days and wait for the bad days to pass, and they will. This too shall pass.

SHARRAN MAKIN

PEARLS OF WISDOM:

Celebrate the good days and wait for the bad days to pass, and they will. (Sharran Makin)

For I know the plans I have for you, declares the lord. Plans to prosper you and not harm you, plans to give you hope and a future. (Jeremiah 29:11)

ABOUT THE AUTHOR

Sharran Makin is a multidisciplinary, national award-winning artist from Lake Macquarie, near Newcastle, NSW. She is best known for her photography, printmaking and painting and loves working with many mediums. Her work is often inspired by nature, the land, and the ocean, which has been an essential part of her life. En plein air art is where she feels most alive and inspired, so you may spot her sketching along a local street, a beach, the lake, the bush, or anywhere outdoors, where she can connect with the land, the people, and her art.

Her work has been exhibited in Newcastle, Lake Macquarie, The Central Coast, Armidale, Mudgee, Maitland and Bathurst. In addition, her art and photography has found its way into many homes and organisations owned by several artists and art collectors. She is also a published author.

SHARRAN MAKIN

She is a member of the Newcastle Urban Sketches, Society of Artists Newcastle, and the Newcastle Printmakers, and teaches workshops.

A significant period of her life was dedicated to serving and protecting the public as an emergency service worker, where she had 14 years of service. She genuinely desires to make people's lives better and this world and her community a better place to live. She also offers art as therapy, mentoring and coaching sessions.

FIND OUT MORE ABOUT THE AUTHOR

If you wish to find out more about the author, view her artwork, find out about upcoming exhibitions or workshops or enquire about public speaking events, please check out her Facebook and Instagram accounts or her website and email.

Website: https://makinartandphotography.com.au/

Facebook: https://www.facebook.com/makinartandphotography

Instagram: https://www.instagram.com/makin_art_and_photography/

Email: makinart101@gmail.com

DISCLAIMER

These are my words; I do not presume to tell another person's story. I am not a medical practitioner; I only advise on what has worked for me and many others, and it may not be suitable for everyone and their unique circumstances. You need to seek your own medical advice. If there is an emergency or someone's life is at risk, you need to call the emergency help phone number for the area in which you live, in Australia, that is 000.

Some other helpful numbers in Australia include:

LIFELINE 13 11 14

BEYOND BLUE 1300 22 4636

NOTES

SHARRAN MAKIN

NOTES

www.ingramcontent.com/pod-product-compliance
Lightning Source LLC
Chambersburg PA
CBHW030037100526
44590CB00011B/239